J P RUFIO: ENTREPRENEUR

An American Success Story

LAURA NADWORNY

RUFIO ENTERPRISES
New York, NY

JP RUFIO: ENTREPRENEUR
An American Success Story

Printed in the United States of America.

RUFIO ENTERPRISES
Suite 667
434 Avenue of the Americas
New York, NY 10011

First Edition

Library of Congress Catalog Card Number: 83-62817

ISBN 0-9612658-0-9

DEDICATION:

To Hazel
who knew JP's special genius
long before the rest of us.

The following memoir is based on actual events, real people & canines. Some names have been changed. But, after all, this is a Dog's life.

NEW YORK POST

By EUGENIA SHEPPARD

Around the Town

* * *

In 14 short years **Rufio** has done it all. Not only is he head of his own T-shirt company for fashion-conscious canines but he is just back from California where he appeared on the Tonight Show.

To celebrate his good fortune, **Rufio** gave a party for himself last night where birthday cake, champagne, cheese and dog biscuits were served to his mixed group of friends. He himself claims no kennel-club rating.

* * *

"A Dog with money is addressed as Mr. Dog."
—Spanish Proverb

Jean Pierre Rufio stood outside the door. He inhaled deeply taking in all the smells and sounds coming through that door. His French good looks were enviable. Strong of limb, he cut a handsome figure in his tuxedo (right off the racks of his latest design collection). He had the culture of a purebred, the intelligence of a French poodle, the build of a construction worker (a short construction worker) and the street smarts of a mutt. He was twenty pounds and a foot & a half long. His full dark hair, now peppered with white, gave him the air of distinction which hard work and determination had earned him. He was, indeed, a complicated personality.

On the other side of that door: a room filled with beings gathered to celebrate his retirement; to honor his achievements as an innovative Captain of Industry and Philanthropist. Most in attendance were groupies: there to be seen with him, to bathe in his limelight. They were members of the press, his lawyers, his accountants, advertising types, models, doctors, his national sales staff, friends, even children (he always felt most simpatico with their joys, their freedoms, their height). They were all there, waiting for him.

JP was a puppy of the 60's. Never a flower dog, he had always padded to a different drummer. His symbol of independence: his Afro-styled coif.

He had grown up thinking "Business" was a dirty word—he was now a successful entrepreneur. Dogs had always been treated as second class citizens—he was now a respected leader in his community. His only regrets were for others: for those friends and associates who, in the final analysis, were not there for him when he needed them most. Oh, he understood it was not because they meant him ill. No, it was because they did not dare to dream. They didn't know how to reach beyond their own self-imposed limitations. If only they could recognize their own potential.

He had come up from obscurity, with no formal education other than six weeks at an obedience school (from which he had characteristically rebelled: he could never deal with those square-peg in square-hole educational theories). Against all odds, he had become an accomplished designer, a manufacturer, an entrepreneur. He had created a product; built an industry. But he had never forgotten his roots.

In this moment of reflection, JP was proud to be a self-made dog . . .

Laura heard him scratching at the door. She looked around at the assembled guests, then opened the door. Leaning toward him, she pinned a red carnation at his lapel. He smelled her delicious perfume (grateful for once the scent did not make him sneeze). She brought his head to hers. They looked into each other's eyes. She was smiling. He nuzzled against her cheek. Proudly she led him into the room.

This was their night: the night they had both worked so hard for all these years. Although he had known her all his life, it was only these last five years which had found them inseparable: as successful business partners and as the best of friends. He had moved in with her back then. She had changed his name. He had changed her life. Although his French macho would not easily admit to it, she was the secret behind all his success. He leaned over and licked her nose. She was his favorite human being.

They glided through the "Bravos!" which filled the room. JP looked around. He was not old enough to be "retiring." He had become bored. Perhaps it was a mid-life crisis. He just needed new challenges. But he did lap up this attention. His whole body wagged. It was like a good piece of cheese: he could never get enough. He gulped it all in.

With his own brand of humility and cool, JP lifted his ears to hear his assembled admirers extol the secret to his success: JP RUFIO was a dog in a dog-eat-dog world.

He raised his front paw for all to admire the retirement watch Laura had just placed on his "wrist." His eyes glistened with pride. He knew what trouble she had gone to to locate just the right timepiece. It had come in a set. He wore the matching one around his tail.

Only in America! Only in America could a French poodle, born in Oregon, raised in America's middle class suburbs, achieve such heights. Tonight he stood proudly on all fours, confident in his role as renaissance canine . . . RUF!

THE EARLY YEARS: NAKED IN THE SUBURBS

> **"Born when the sun is in Aries, you are pioneering, headstrong and impulsive. Full of ambition, you love new ideas and enterprises. You have tremendous enthusiasm, persistence and will power . . . Nobody bosses you around; you'd much rather be at the head of your own organization or at least leading the field in some new endeavor. You have a great love of justice, freedom and individual determination . . ."**
>
> **—Joseph F. Goodavage**
> **"Write Your Own Horoscope"**
> **Signet 1979**

Born in the environmentally sound state of Oregon, under the sign of Aries, JP was ripped from his mother at birth. Sold into a suburban Westchester County human clan, he was immediately shipped East.

Diana, the younger daughter in this eastern family, had anxiously awaited the day her older sister, Laura, would go off to college so she could replace her with a puppy dog. Roget, a miniature French poodle, was Laura's replacement. The whole family adored him. Roget was perfect.

But tragedy struck. Roget had been trained to come to a whistle. On that fateful day, that whistle lured him back home, across the street. A car sped up the road. There was a screech of wheels. Then, silence. Roget was dead. The family was in mourning. JP was brought in as Roget's replacement.

JP was met with the awesome responsibility of turning this depressed family around: an incredible challenge—a public relations job if ever there was one. He knew he could do it. Hearing the folklore of the "perfect" Roget, again and again and again, JP recognized the need to develop a style all his own. There would be no room in his life for the limitations of perfection.

The next problem to confront JP was his name. How could he, who always had to have a leg up on everything, he who suffered from such a strong case of macho, how could he operate with a French poodle name like "Jean Pierre Chiffon?" Who would take him seriously? Who could carry that label around day-in and day-out? He demanded a "real" dog's name. His choice: "JP." "JP" reflected all that he was and would become. It took him a while, but he did train the family to call him "JP." That was only the beginning of this family's training.

* * *

JP had not yet broken them of all of their Roget patterns. Diana, who had learned to love JP as much as she had Roget, dared to enroll JP in the same discipline school that Roget had attended (where, of course, Roget had been teacher's pet). Throughout his six weeks of instruction, JP was an obedient student. He did try to live up to expectations. But during his graduation ceremony, he took significant steps toward independence.

Diana walked JP around the gym for the final class exercise. A hush fell over the anxious relatives who watched from atop the packed bleachers. Even Laura, who was home on school vacation, and who never took the whole obedience school "thing" too seriously, watched with proud anticipation. Diana led JP around the assigned circle. She stopped, dropped the leash and stood perfectly still. She was well trained. JP dutifully went through his paces. He sat down. He looked up at Diana and yawned. Boredom glazed his eyes. He looked around for a way out.

At that moment, up in the bleachers, Laura, almost inaudibly, whispered: "JP come here." JP's head tilted in Laura's direction. "JP come here."

Like a shot, JP leaped to his escape. He bounded up the bleachers into Laura's lap. Diana was left holding the leash. The gym filled with anarchistic glee. JP licked Laura's face vigorously: Free at last! Free at last!

"Meat never hangs so high but a dog will try his legs."
—Spanish Proverb

Early in his life, JP, for very practical reasons, developed an appreciation for music. Like all poodles, he would sing when continually howled at by his human masters. JP did find this human howling a peculiar ritual. But watching an adult human lift his face to the skies, round out his mouth and hoot like a Basset hound in heat, cracked him up every time. And because JP always appreciated a good laugh, he usually accommodated himself to this odd activity. But this was not his taste in music.

JP taught himself to play the piano. This kind of music made more sense. It had its rewards. Chocolates were often left on top of the upright piano (put there, of course, to be out of his reach as he cruised the living room). Because JP's nose was a finely honed instrument, he recognized an appetizing smell wherever there was one.

Overcoming his initial fear of heights, as well as the fright caused by the unexpected melodies underfoot, he padded his way to the top of the piano. He learned quickly to tickle the ivories so that the chocolates could tickle his tummy.

Except for this chocolate fetish, JP never considered himself much of a gourmet. He was very clear about this. His was a palate of the common dog. From day one it was cheese. Cheese, in fact, was his greatest earthly delight. He would do almost anything for a piece of cheese. It was his reward and his tranquilizer. It was also the only way to escape him. For anyone who dared to leave him behind, the only way out was a piece of cheese thrown in the opposite direction of the exit. JP would always go for the cheese. Escape was a breeze. Cheese was JP's Achilles heel.

JP picked up certain habits on those suburban streets which were to serve him well in his climb up the ladder of success. He learned to express himself, to speak his mind. Outdoors most of the day, JP's natural wanderlust was curbed by his involuntary attachment to a chain run on the side of the house. Being stuck on that chain isolated him from the action on the street. JP had to find a way to bring it all to him. He used the only thing he had working for him: his bark. Through the constant use of his voice, he not only made himself the center of neighborhood attention, but he also rid himself of his accent: the squeak of the poodle. He, in fact, achieved the ultimate for his sniping breed: his bark really did become worse than his bite.

* * *

Whenever possible, JP did manage to squeeze out of his chained collar to enjoy some limited freedom as well as to tryst with one female neighbor or another. An especially easy time to slip away was right after he had been groomed. But in the early days, groomers had their way with JP. He often ended up looking like . . . a poodle! The problem with freedom at this point, was that JP felt so ridiculous being this clean shaven, that he was too ashamed to show his body in the neighborhood. So the neighborhood came to him. On any given sunny day, there would be JP, hooked up to his six yard run. And there would be the line-up: a collie, a boxer, a Doberman and a couple of mutts, all female, all waiting for their moment in the sun!

* * *

JP's need for creative and intellectual expression, as exemplified by his Afro'd hair, made groomers the enemy. He doggedly drove them up the cage wall.

He instantly established his territory upon entering any hair salon. He refused to wait his turn in a poodle-sized cage. He let his groomers know, in no uncertain terms, that closed quarters were not his thing. His nonstop barking in these anxious moments of captivity, not only strengthened his voice, it got the whole pet shop talking/ chirping/ barking/ meowing/ swimming. The groomers learned. JP was given the run of the place. As JP's public image became more important, so did his groomers. No longer could they take chances at ruffling his feathers. He was becoming an acknowledged trendsetter: if he looked good, they looked good.

* * *

After JP had been living with his adopted family for several years, Diana went off to college. The family would not let her take JP with her. So, when she did come back, which was only to visit, she brought a new friend: the sleek and beautiful Albion Moonlight. Albie, a black Labrador retriever, was a laid-back Vermont gentledog. JP was furious. First of all, Albie had taken Diana from him. (JP could be very possessive.) And now, this Albie dog was on JP's turf. The little guy did not like that at all. JP, like many short people, could get very Napoleonic.

* * *

JP's home and his life were about to change. He was about to be uprooted from the suburbs, from the family, from his female amoureux. Laura had returned to take him with her to New York City. JP perceived Laura as his freedom as well as his responsibility. Laura was crazy about him. Whenever she came home (she lived and worked in New York) she spent most of her visit playing with "The Kid," as she liked to call him. Now that her parents were moving to Florida and Diana was busy with Albie, Laura could take JP for her own.

In a trial weekend visit to the Big Apple, JP, left to his own devices, transformed a beautiful green rug into piles of deformed green spaghetti. Laura, who was not very well trained, had forgotten his cheese. JP attempted to dig his way out of his carpeted jail. Laura returned home to find him strangling in his own spaghetti. The cheese was never forgotten again. JP and Laura would live in rugless splendor.

This move was an awesome adjustment for both of them. Typically, JP did not merely rise to the occasion, he turned it to his advantage.

THE WINTER OF HIS DISCONTENT

JP, settled into his new home, epitomized the urbanized country dog. Set aside, but not far beneath the surface, were his memories of those lazy naked days, lying out on his lawn gulping in the glorious sunlight, contemplating the wonders of nature. Left behind were those fresh delicious smells, the casual visits with canine neighbors. In their place, the frenzied city life. The lawns were now paved with tar and filled with loud, huge vehicles. And the air tasted bad.

Like his city cousins, JP was confined to a leash whenever he walked Laura. The other city dogs were not very friendly. They all seemed in too much of a hurry. JP spent more and more time indoors, in their little Greenwich Village studio apartment. He paced. He was distracted. He reread his favorites: "Eloise at the Plaza;" "Happiness is a Warm Puppy;" Machiavelli's "The Prince;" all of Jerry Brown's political speeches and back issues of National Geographic. Woody Allen wasn't funny anymore. John Lennon was too much a mirror of times past. Only Billy Joel came closest to expressing JP's own raw restlessness.

What was happening to him? Could this be it? Had he, Jean Pierre Chiffon, already tasted the best that life had to offer him at such an early age? Was he old before his time? Was it true that you can't teach an old dog new tricks? Was there any reason to go on? How could Laura have done this to him?

Winter came. Their walks outside were shorter and less frequent. JP used to love to play in the snow. But here, even the snow was grim and dirty. The streets were now covered with stinging salt. He had never felt so low. One day, through his depressed stupor, he noticed something incredible. All the dogs were wearing . . . clothes???

JP had never seen animals in people's clothing before. It blew his mind. For the first time in months he had a good laugh. How absurd. What a weird place this New York City was! JP was beginning to love it.

Pulling himself up to his full height, recovering his composure long enough to place tongue in cheek, JP muttered to himself: They might as well be wearing t-shirts. His own thoughts stopped him in his tracks. T-Shirts for dogs? T-SHIRTS FOR DOGS!

JP's mind was speeding. He felt alive again. What had been the symbol of human rebellion in the 60's, could make the same statement for the canines of the 70's. (Heaven only knows they needed some inspiration.) From the depths of his despair, JP had risen to the heights of artistry. JP had just created the Original T-Shirt for Dogs!

In one blustery winter moment, JP was his old self again. He cackled, not imagining that this inside joke with himself would lead him laughing all the way to the bank. JP's life would never be the same.

> **"Whatever you can do or dream you can, begin it. Boldness has genius, power and magic in it."**
> **—Goethe**

JP was now copping a peak at every Women's Wear Daily and Vogue Magazine he could get his paws on. He had fashion on the brain. (Once he had fought Laura when she tied a wet Handiwipe around his neck to keep him cool. Now he was demanding silk.) JP was thinking "Collection."

But he was in conflict with himself. He padded around his apartment; barking, snarling, whining, mumbling to himself. He was still not philosophically comfortable about preaching dog clothes. No "real" canine needed them. Besides, clothes inhibited movement. And in this world, you have to be ready to move. He worried about his brother and sister canines, especially these city dogs. They were much too willing to please the master race. They were too acquiescent. Geez, how that irritated him! And clothes were surely the ultimate symbol of this submission to human "cute."

* * *

His creative energies were going wild—his heart was unsure. Doing his own thing, expressing himself, was one thing. But becoming a business? After all, he was emphatically opposed to multinational corporations and the powers they brokered. Big money scared him. It can change anyone's perspective, even someone as in touch with himself and his priorities as JP. JP was nervous that he was moving dangerously close to selling out. He had seen it happen again and again to other activist breeds of the 60's: the Black Panthers, the White Yippies.

Finally, JP made his decision: he would surrender his heart and his mind to this brainchild of his. But he promised himself no matter what his accomplishments, he would remember his brothers and sisters. It was a commitment JP never did forget.

* * *

JP now had to figure out how to become a business. The first thing he did was to take Laura into his confidence. (You have to trust somebody.) JP broke the first rule of business: never go into business with a friend or relative. He decided to take the chance. Aside from being wrapped around JP's little paw, Laura also had legitimate professional qualifications: she knew the media and had experience in the fashion world. In fact, she had the perfect training to be his assistant designer of dog t-shirts: she was a graduate of the famous Parsons School of Design. And, because she had worked in the garment industry, she spoke their language: dog-eat-dog.

JP sat up on his hind legs and begged. It worked every time. She loved him. They were partners.

Within months, JP's job description would go from simply "mad dog with idea" to one which included everything from innovator to entrepreneur to manager of the lawyers, the accountants, sales and distribution, printing, factories, promotion, advertising, package design, marketing, to media star. But in the beginning, while he tried to figure out what all the pieces were and how to bring them together (neither he nor Laura had any formal business schooling), JP felt less like a C.E.O. and more like a Rockette kicking in mud.

Rufio Says:

Red Fleece Sweatshirt

Terrycloth TankTop

Swedish Bicycle Jacket

Rugby

JOG

Tuxedo

THE COLLECTION

JP knew the look and fit he wanted his t-shirts to have. And he drove Laura up the wall trying to achieve it. He was a rotten model, not able to sit still for any period of time. Laura kept sticking him with pins, accidentally, but repeatedly. JP did not like that at all. More often than not, he found himself biting the hand that fed him. Laura threatened to stuff him and market him. But when the t-shirt was finished, JP strutted and purred. His bowed, hairy front legs jutted out of the sleeves, tough and macho. JP's t-shirt was a chic French t-shirt: the body clung tight; the hemline stopped just past his waist. He was the cat's meow. If only the girls from the old neighborhood could see him now!

Their first ready-to-wear collection was finished. It was a smashing line of T-shirts for Dogs. Each shirt had a screenprinted JP paw print where an alligator might otherwise go. The JP designer label stuck out from the shoulder seam. All designs were printed on the back of the shirt, of course.

FOR THAT CANINE PHYSIQUE . . .

RUFIO®s T-SHIRT SIZE CHART

"If you call a tail a leg, how many legs has a dog? Five? No. Calling a tail a leg, don't make it a leg."
—Abraham Lincoln

JP and Laura were giddy with exhaustion from their all-night brainstorming sessions. They were smugly savoring their inspirations when it dawned on them: all dogs do not wear JP's size. JP did not want to sell his collection to a limited market. He wanted it available to the world.

They sent away for size charts. They looked in pet stores at the sweaters and coats. None of these things helped. Dog clothes were based on neck-to-tail measurements. One beautiful chart offered pictures of hundreds of breeds but only pointed out the differences, not the similarities, in weight, height and length. There existed no standardized sizes for dogs.

* * *

The more involved JP became with his new venture, the greater was his need to get outdoors, to break away from the confinements of his apartment. Those walls made him feel like a caged animal. To relieve that tension, he took lots of walks. He was beginning to adjust to city life. He was learning to appreciate the fire hydrants and parked car tires. Trees were a dim and fading memory.

During one of those walks, this one taken to try to escape the mental burdens of dog sizing, JP and Laura passed by a lady being escorted by her two mutts. Both dogs were larger than JP. Both were different sizes. Without thinking twice about how she would be received, Laura addressed the human being.

Gesturing unconsciously to include JP: "We are developing a new product for dogs. I would appreciate it if you would let me measure and fit your two dogs?"

The woman inched backwards. The two dogs sniffed JP.

"Would you mind meeting us here tomorrow at about noon?"

"Sure," the woman mumbled, smiled nervously then hurriedly dragged her companions away.

Laughing at herself, Laura squatted down next to her short partner: "She thought I was nuts!"

JP licked her face and barked.

Courage grows with repetition. Having done it once and having survived feeling like a fool, Laura asked every dog and human couple they passed that day. She got the same reaction from everyone. She did not believe for a minute that any of them would show up for the fitting.

Noon the next day, JP led the hesitating Laura by his leash toward the appointed spot at Sixth Avenue and 12th Street. She was convinced they would be greeted by no one. They turned the corner and stopped dead in their tracks. They could not believe their eyes.

The word had spread. There at the corner was a crowd of dogs. Most of them had not been invited. But there they all were, lined up, waiting to be measured. Laura winked at JP: "And they think we're crazy."

* * *

Figuring out the sizing was agonizing, dreary work. The partners ended up agreeing on a four size spread: xs-s-m-l. But that was the least of it. There were unexpected considerations. JP had to admit that he had never given much thought to whether Dobermans had skinny legs or that retrievers had thick necks or even whether Yorkshire terriers came in three sizes. What a diversified and fascinating race he came from.

When the patterns were finally completed, JP decided to devise his own size chart for customer reference. He wanted to make his customers comfortable so they would not be afraid to try this new product. After all, dogs had never before worn t-shirts. He also wanted his t-shirts to appeal to those dogs out there who, like himself, had never worn any clothes. The size chart was good public relations.

But the sizing problems did not end there. JP began getting calls at all hours of the night:

"It's too small for my Pomeranian."

"It's too big for my Chihuahua."

"My Yorkie doesn't like red."

"My German shepherd loves it, but now that he has it on, I forced it on him, it really was too small for him, he won't let me take it off."

It was at this time that JP bought his first piece of office equipment: a telephone answering machine. The size chart was adjusted and so were the sizes. JP made an addition to this new chart: a policy statement about the importance of the quality and proper fit of his t-shirts.

"The dog who has a friend for an attorney, is a fool of a client."

—JP Hotdog

Despite his highly developed social consciousness and his hyperactive creative curiosity, JP was naive in the ways of the business world. One group for which he held idealized expectations was lawyers. This was understandable since his only exposure to the law had been through his own activism. He had been inspired by a speech given by an activst attorney at Harvard in the early 70's. This lawyer's commitment to the underdog had profoundly affected JP. And through attorneys like Ralph Nader, who were committed to the rights of the consumer, JP learned what it meant to work like a dog for what you believed in. So how could JP know what lay ahead in the world of corporate law?

JP's t-shirt line was finished: the styles selected, the fabrics chosen, the designer label created, the screenprinting designed and the sizing set. Now was the time to make it all legal. Before he could make his collection public, he had to protect himself. He had to incorporate, register his trademarks and copyright his patterns.

Lawyer #1 was hired to incorporate them. Choosing the corporate name was choosing an image. "Dog T-Shirt Company" would not do. JP rejected lists and lists of names. Finally he had it: JP & MOONLIGHT, ltd.

Why "Moonlight?" You remember Albie, the Vermont gentledog, who took over JP's place in Diana's heart? His full name is Albion Moonlight. And, although JP never admitted it out loud (too much pride), he truly admired Albie's quiet grace and wisdom. His name on

ALBION MOONLIGHT

the company would be good karma. Besides, Albie had the one thing JP could never have again, Diana.

The name went through its corporate search with no problems. There was nowhere in the land another JP & MOONLIGHT, ltd. JP was now a business.

* * *

Lawyer #1, quick to recognize the money-making potential of the t-shirts, offered to invest in the business. JP was too flattered. He did not even stop to consider the potential problems of this partnership. He saw it only as a vote of confidence. Lawyer #1 soon began to undermine his own good works.

One of these first "good works" was to recommend a patent attorney, Lawyer #2, for the purpose of registering JP & MOONLIGHT's trademarks ("JP" and JP's pawprint) and copyrighting the patterns, which were original in concept as well as creation to JP.

Lawyer #2 counselled JP to immediately proceed with his manufacturing plans, using his selected trademarks. JP had no reason to question his advice. (If you don't know the right answers, you can't ask the right questions.) JP knew nothing about copyright law. And, of course, assumed if a lawyer told him to do it, then it was okay to do it.

Fabric labels were made, screens for printing were completed, promotional items (buttons, bumper stickers) were manufactured.

Fortunately for him, JP had some friends who had more business savvy than he did. One of these friends, a heavy-duty legal beagle, questioned how quickly a trademark search had been done. What trademark search? JP got on the phone with Lawyer #2, Laura called Lawyer #1. Everything was halted. Lucky for JP & MOONLIGHT, ltd. that no fabric had been printed, no shirts sewn. A mistake like this could wipe out an untested business before its product ever got to market. As it was, five weeks of production were lost and several hundred dollars went down the drain. But, because the product had not yet been introduced onto the marketplace, its credibility was not undermined.

JP was furious. He could not stop his own barking. His Afro stood on end. He grabbed for his favorite blanket and started thrashing it about. He clenched one end in his mouth and squatted down on his belly. His back legs jutted out flat on the floor behind him. He clamped the rest of the blanket with his front paws and ripped away. He jumped up and whipped, what was now a rag, at Laura. His jaws were locked around the rag like a vice. She grabbed at the loose end. His tough little twenty pound body swept Laura clear across the room. JP was fighting mad. This was just the beginning of JP's dealings with incompetence. He did not take to it very well.

When confronted with all this, Lawyer #1 (who was then a partner) shrugged his shoulders irresponsibly and told JP to find another patent attorney. JP snapped at him, ripping his Pierre Cardin pant leg.

> **"The first thing we do, let's kill all the lawyers."**
> **—Shakespeare (King Henry VI Pt. 2)**

A new patent attorney was found. Lawyer #3 was from the old school, always striving for excellence. Thorough and considerate of his clients, Mark even took the time to teach Laura how to make a preliminary trademark search in the public library. This saved time and money. But all their problems were not solved. And it was Laura who had to break the news to JP. The name "JP" was already registered to someone else. Could there really be another JP?

JP, doggedly determined to be positive, put Laura right to work searching out another name. He had already gone through one name change in his life. This would not be an easy adjustment. This new name had to encompass all the goals, dreams and attitudes he was building into his business. JP waivered between a poetic, flowing name or a tough screws-to-the-wall image-making name. He scoured baby books, record albums, telephone directories, history texts and cheap paperback romances. You name it, he considered it.

Mark, Lawyer #3, provided him with a government listing of names. The names were listed in English and then translated into a dozen or so foreign languages. JP was tantalized by the intrigue of something foreign sounding (after all, he was a poodle "Français"). But what he discovered was not French. It was Italian. It was perfect. Even back in 1976, JP knew that Milan was fast becoming the new fashion capital of the world. He had his new name: RUFIO, pronounced RUF I O. It had just enough "RUF" to signify a designer of dog clothes. Translated it was Rufus, which means redhead. And Laura was a redhead!

So, Jean Pierre Chiffon of Medford, Oregon, by way of Briarcliff, New York, became JP RUFIO, creator of RUFIO®s CANINE CLASSIC®, the Original T-Shirt for Dogs . . . RUF!

L
XU
BNN
VSXP

"Plus je vois les hommes, plus j'admire les chiens."
—Mme. Roland

On his street walks, JP sized up more than just lines of dogs. One day, positioned in a concentrated squat near the curb, JP spotted a lovely young female human walking toward him. She was on her way to the next corner. He fixed his gaze upon her. She glanced toward him. Their eyes connected. Leaving Laura to clean up after him, JP jumped onto the sidewalk and waited for this enchantress to pet him as she passed by. She didn't pet him. She waved and said: "Hi!" JP's tail was speeding. He watched, wondering when it would dawn on the girl that she had just waved to a dog?

* * *

JP never wanted to outgrow the puppy in him. He loved to giggle. He would sit up with one back leg stretched perpendicularly out to his side, tilt his head and bark sweetly. He was, in those moments, irresistible. Laura would sit down next to him and he would cuddle in so close to her, you couldn't tell where he stopped and she started. With his front paw, he would reach for her hand and pull it to his belly. Then he would roll over for the next best thing since his "ladies of the lawn:" a tummy rub. All semblance of orneriness melted away.

* * *

JP's emerging role as an entrepreneurial dog did demand that he exercise certain restraints, including keeping his quick temper under control. But sometimes . . .

Jason, a magnificent Great Dane, lived in the same apartment building as JP. They met often on the elevator and out on the street. They frequented the same fire hydrants. JP would look up at Jason with a mischievous glint in his eye. He secretly wanted to ride the giant Dane off into the sunset. (JP had never seen a real horse.)

One day Jason and his human came to visit JP. Laura, assuming JP would be pleased, invited them in.

JP was uncharacteristically quiet during the visit. He sat rigidly at the other end of the room. He never took his eyes off his viking friend. His own home seemed suddenly too small for him. Jason began to sniff around. Laura let him have free reign. Why not? He was a friend. JP never moved within three feet of the Dane. He began pulling at his bones and rags. Jason sniffed on. JP watched him like a hawk. Jason gracefully pranced over to a standing sculpture, appropriately titled "Copper Tree." He sniffed it. He circled it. He sniffed again. He gracefully lifted his leg. He watered the tree. He created an indoor lake.

Jason's human was appropriately horrified. JP just sat. He watched. Laura moved into action. The lake was drained. The flooded area and the sculpture were wiped around with ammonia to eliminate any signal. Jason and his human made a swift and apologetic exit. JP watched.

He stood up. He began circling. And circling. And circling. He never said a word. He never barked. He kept circling. Each circle brought him closer and closer to the "Copper Tree." Abruptly he stopped. He fixed his icy gaze upon the tree. A growl from deep in the pit of his stomach filled the room. JP violently threw up all over the "Copper Tree."

Jason was not invited back . . . RUF!

JP was hardly ever anti-social. He liked people and dogs and loved to party. He was a good friend to have.

He did have certain human favorites. In fact, except for his harem of admiring and alluring female canines, and his best friends Gus & Shonie (two Dobermans who had padded their way to Nashville to seek their fame and fortune), JP did seem to prefer human company. He learned fast that humans were malleable. His brothers would never allow him to get away with half the stuff that people did. But neither were they nearly so supportive of his need to achieve. Oh, it wasn't that his dog friends were lazy (it would be human laziness which would later devastate JP), the canines were just not interested. Their horizons had been limited by their leashed-in lives. They had trouble connecting with JP's need to reach beyond his own backyard.

One of his favorites was a human female who was also his business consultant. She was always there to help him out. But JP sensed that she was sometimes afraid of dogs. JP believed that in her case, it was just a lack of exposure, not a deep-seated prejudice. So he tried to be on his best behavior when she was around.

One night, to show his appreciation, he left a bunch of daisies at her door. He didn't want to disturb her by barking. Several hours later, while taking Laura for a walk, JP spotted her with some of her human friends. She turned to her friends, matter-of-factly pointing toward JP and informed them, with great delight, that that was the dog who had sent her the flowers. She didn't notice the strange looks that crossed her friends' faces. JP's tail was going.

"Every amateur thinks; I could have done it as well."
—W.H. Auden ("Epistle to a Godson & Other Poems")

JP did stumble around on the way to his success. Making the business work was like putting together pieces of a demented jigsaw puzzle.

He was a pushover for innovative concepts. If you threw him an idea, he would go for it the way he would a good piece of cheese. He was also a magnet, attracting information and contacts from unexpected sources. This had him padding in twenty directions at once. He was like a sponge. He learned fast. He instinctively knew how to make things happen.

But this did not make him immune to the callous, jealous statements of others. Strangers would approach him on the street and smugly inform him that they had had a much better idea than his silly t-shirts. (This always seemed to happen when JP had been up all night working on his "silly" product.) Politely he would inquire about what they had done with their sure-fire concepts. "Oh nothing, yet. It's still in my desk drawer. But someday . . ." The first few times this happened JP's feelings were hurt. But he learned to ignore these closet innovators. He was out there putting his tail on the line. And he was loving it . . .

THE GOOD OLE DOG NETWORK

JP knew there was more to making a business happen than just hard work. As much as he hated this piece of the puzzle, he understood it and somehow accepted it: success was not just dependent on what you knew, it was also who you knew. That Good Ole Dog Network could be very effective.

There he was, at the corner of 55th Street and the Avenue of the Americas, portfolio in teeth, pacing back and forth. JP had an appointment with a big shot manufacturer, a friend of a friend, who was going to help JP & MOONLIGHT find a factory to produce the t-shirts. JP's whole body was tense. Oh, it wasn't because he was meeting 'The Man.' No, it was something else. JP wasn't wearing anything. Laura and he had agreed: until the t-shirts were presented to the public it would be better if he did not wear them outside the apartment, so he would not encourage the copy cats. But JP had been wearing his t-shirt around the house so much lately that now standing on a corner in midtown Manhattan, he felt naked without it.

A gleaming golden Rolls-Royce was luxuriating its way up the avenue toward JP. It was 'The Man's office-away-from-the-office. The chauffeur pulled the car over to the sidewalk and opened the door. From the back seat 'The Man' beckoned JP to enter. He jumped in, climbed up on the seat next to 'The Man' and opened his brief case. JP was all business. 'The Man,' he was cool.

As the Rolls sleeked its way across 55th Street and down Seventh Avenue, 'The Man' poured himself a Scotch. He offered JP a drink: water on the rocks in a bowl. JP gulped in the car's glitzy interior as fast as he did his drink. He studied 'The Man.' He was short, like JP. JP was impressed.

JP held up his end of the conversation. He was learning to wheel and deal. He had made his t-shirt patterns so that the sewing per garment would be as inexpensive as possible (the fewer seams, the cheaper the cost). He was here looking for the right price. He did not mind using a non-union shop.

Had he really come to this? JP had always been pro-worker/ pro-union/ pro-American goods. As his hard work evolved into a reality, he was uncompromising in his goal to offer the best product he could at the most reasonable price. He was more committed to product quality at fair prices than to holding on to some empty archaic ideals. He had always assumed that the union worker would provide this quality. It hurt him to learn otherwise.

'The Man' offered him his factory in Rockland County, New York and another in Pennsylvania. He held out his hand to JP to close the deal. JP stared blankly at him.

"Agreed?"

JP did not budge.

'The Man' grew exasperated. "Shake?"

That JP understood. He was not trained to do many tricks, but shaking hands was one he knew. The command was "Shake." 'The Man' had said the word. JP offered his right paw. 'The Man' shook it and let go. JP, uncharacteristically Pavlovian, automatically offered his left paw . . . The pressure was getting to him.

The chauffeur maneuvered the Rolls back up Sixth Avenue to the 55th Street corner. With the deal consummated, the meeting was over. The chauffeur dutifully opened the door. JP was let out of the car. He stood on the corner watching the Rolls as it disappeared up the avenue. JP had his first introduction to his own ambition. That manufacturer was leading a real dog's life.

The first batch of t-shirts arrived from the factory just in time for a scheduled meeting with department store buyers. JP could not wait to try one. He ripped into the carton. Laura helped him on with the new green JOG shirt. He let out a piercing howl as he thrust his paw into one of the sleeves. The armhole was too tight. It hurt him so much he nearly bit Laura as she pulled him out of it. What had happened?

All the samples had fit perfectly. The paper patterns used to cut the t-shirts were made from those samples. Why didn't it fit him? JP went for his rag. He was so upset. He could not deal with it. Laura examined the new shirt. She took it apart and compared it to the original patterns. The bodies matched perfectly. So did the sleeves. What was wrong? She studied another shirt. The sleeves had been sewn in backwards. The narrower hemline (which should have been at the dog's elbow) had been sewn into the shoulder seam. They checked through the carton. Every shirt was the same. JP was howling. Laura was on the phone to 'The Man.'

He told her, without hearing her out, that it was JP's fault. He was just a novice. He had obviously made a mistake in the patterns. Patronizingly he assured her that such mistakes were bound to happen, JP had never been in business before. Besides, JP was only a dog, what could you expect?

JP knew prejudice and chauvinism when he heard it. The next day the partners drove over the Tappan Zee Bridge to the Rockland County factory. Their arrival was met with armed resistance. 'The Man's arrogance was slick. He tried to soothe JP by telling him that even though the mistake was, of course, JP's, he would make all the corrections (and just bill JP for the work). JP was foaming at the mouth.

Laura, in the meantime, had taken apart shirts in all sizes to compare them to the original patterns. No way was she going to let 'The Man' blame JP for something that was not his fault. She proved, in every case, that the patterns were right and the sewing was wrong. In the midst of this uproar, Laura called their other partner, Lawyer #1, for some consoling. She should have known better.

"You don't need my help. You can handle it. 'The Man' is probably right. He knows more than you do. So just be nice and let him help you."

Laura went to the rag . . . RUF!

THE LABEL DROP CAPER

JP examined the shirts once more before leaving. He could not believe what he found: another mistake. The designer labels, which jutted out from the shoulder seams, were sewn in wrong. The right side of the label, with the RUFIO pawprint, was supposed to face up as the dog wore it. All the labels were sewn in, face down. Again, 'The Man' blamed it on JP. He confidently assured them that the samples given to the factory to copy from, had the labels sewn in the wrong way and the factory workers had copied those samples exactly.

A factory worker brought over those samples. The designer labels were sewn in properly. 'The Man' was wrong again. And again, he offered to make the correction. But the factory would need more labels.

It was 4 PM Friday afternoon. If JP waited to bring the new labels to the factory on Monday, he might not get the shirts back until the following week. With all those buyers' appointments set, time was of the

"He's not trying to catch his tail... he's looking for the designer label on his new sweater."

essence. JP and Laura decided to deliver the labels that same evening.

Because the factory would be all locked up by the time they returned, 'The Man' instructed them to throw the boxes of labels behind a bush for safekeeping. (The factory was in a very rough neighborhood.) 'The Man' would come by in the morning and retrieve them.

JP, 'The Man' and Laura trotted out to the front of the building. Slyly, 'The Man' looked around. He silently pointed to a bush. JP sniffed it and then lifted his leg. 'The Man,' unamused, selected another shrub.

JP and Laura collapsed into the car. Exhausted, they drove over the Tappan Zee Bridge, into Manhattan, found a parking spot, picked up the labels, got back in the car and again drove over the bridge. They arrived at the factory after dark. Laura checked out the area, then cautiously stepped out of the car. She was really too tired to be playing "I Spy." She looked around and then, acting as if she was just out for a stroll, approached the building. She placed the boxes of labels behind the appointed bush and skulked back to the car. For the fourth time that day she was driving across the Hudson River. JP curled up and slept the whole trip home.

Within two days the newly sewn shirts were delivered to JP. 'The Man' removed himself from their arrangement. JP would now deal exclusively with the Pennsylvania factory. JP was about ready to meet his public.

. . . UP TO HIS EARS IN DOG SHIRT(S)

Screenprinted t-shirts were the human vogue of the day. RUFIO's CANINE CLASSICS would uphold that tradition. Some shirts would have sayings, some would have designs, all would have the RUFIO pawprint. In his enthusiasm to create the screens and find a good screenprinter, JP forgot to consider the logistics.

First the fabric had to be cut, then the pieces to be printed had to be shipped to the printer then back to the factory to be sewn. Because JP had the fabric selected and cut long before he found a screenprinter, the factory shipped the cut goods, all 100 dozen, to his apartment.

When JP finally found a screenprinter, he had to taxi the t-shirts to the printer's factory himself. Next time, it would be different . . .

Screenprinter #1 was a real prince charming. He smoothly won JP's trust. He gave JP a tour of his factory, patiently explaining step by step what screenprinting was and the numerous design possibilities it afforded him. JP was so intrigued he thought he might even like to try his paw at it when he had some free time. Screenprinter #1 costed out JP's needs and quoted a price. All this was verbally agreed upon.

JP delivered the cut goods and did not see them again until the finished t-shirts were delivered to him by the Pennsylvania factory. Screenprinter #1 had done a nice, clean job. The bill came. JP & MOONLIGHT had been charged twice the agreed upon price. JP went to his rag. Laura went to argue with the printer.

Screenprinter #2 came highly recommended by several human t-shirt manufacturers. This order was put in writing. JP was launching his most intricate screen to date: the tuxedo t-shirt. It required two screens: one for the tuxedo and one for the red carnation at the lapel. JP was really excited about this shirt.

The first carton arrived. JP could hardly contain himself while Laura opened the box. Oh, no. They could not believe it. The shirts were a disaster. It was not just that the red carnations were painted black, or that the bow tie was printed on sideways. The white cotton knit shirts were smeared and streaked as if they had been used to clean paint brushes. JP did not have to go to his rag; he had a box full of them. What was equally incomprehensible was that the Pennsylvania factory had received this garbage and had sewn the shirts anyway, which meant JP had to pay for them.

JP itemized everything, consuming a couple of pounds of cheese in the process. He not only charged Screenprinter #2 back for the screenprinting, but also for the sewing as well as the cloth. JP was a bear. He kept at them until he got every penny back.

Screenprinter #3 was recommended to JP & MOONLIGHT by a former tennis pro . . . JP, traumatized from his past two experiences, hounded Screenprinter #3 at every step. His work was clean and always on time. His price was excellent. JP relaxed.

The phone rang. It was Pennsylvania. They had just received another shipment of the rugby stripe t-shirts from Screenprinter #3, who had now been printing reorders for this, JP's most popular style, for at least three months. This time they had printed the RUFIO pawprint on the wrong side of the fabric. The factory wanted to know if they should sew them anyway. JP was now pulling out every rag and bone in his repertoire. He was growling like a German shepherd. Laura was starting to fancy the window ledge.

Screenrpinter #3 whined: "Don't get mad at me. How am I supposed to know which is the right side or the wrong side?"

But you've been printing these shirts for three months.

"I guess I was just lucky those other times."

RUF! RUF! RUF!

"A Dog is not insulted when called a Dog."
—West African Proverb

JP was determined that nothing sidetrack him from achieving the high quality product he would be proud to put his name on. His energies were very focused. He knew his demands were irritating. He knew out there, on Seventh Avenue, they were calling him a son of a bitch. But where he came from, that was no insult. He was sticking to his goals: top quality at reasonable prices. He would not sell out.

By using Monsanto textiles, JP was allowed to submit his t-shirts for durability testing by the Monsanto laboratories. JP's hounding of his contractors paid off. The t-shirts passed with flying colors. JP added this final touch to his collection: RUFIO's CANINE CLASSIC the Original T-Shirt for Dogs would carry the Monsanto WearDated Label.

"Dogs begin in jest and end in earnest."
—Proverb

JP (naked) and Laura (dressed) packed up a few samples and were off to see a friend of Laura's who was the manager of a local boutique. It was time for a practice run. JP, more hyper than usual, stopped at every tire along their five block walk. It became a very long walk. When they finally arrived, JP jumped up on the counter and sat quietly.

Laura took the tie-dyed "earth" shirt out and began to pull it over JP's head. They had done this hundreds of times. JP opened his mouth, blocking the shirt from moving down his neck. He chomped down on it: instant lock jaw. Laura looked toward the manager and gave a half smile.

"Come on, JP." She gently tugged at the shirt.

Curious store customers gathered around. Laura pulled a little harder. JP's eyes were glistening with determination and laughter. He was very pleased with himself.

"Why are you doing this to me?"

"Because it's dumb to put clothes on a dog," one customer chimed in.

Laura was now nose to nose with The Kid: "See what you've started?" She growled, "Let go."

She tugged. He pulled. She tried sweet talking him; she tried scolding; she did some more tugging. Nothing worked. JP held his ground.

Laura, in the interest of business, admitted defeat. She reached into her bag with her free hand and whispered: 'Cheese." JP let go of the "earth" shirt . . . RUF!

"A package any dog would be proud to carry home in his mouth."
—JP RUFIO

JP had always assumed that his t-shirts would come in a package especially designed for them. It had to present the t-shirt in a stylish manner and be appealing all by itself. He created a chic RUFIO bag of clear plastic with RUFIO pawprints running diagonally across. Black handles snapped it shut. JP was very pleased. This was no ordinary doggie bag. But something more was needed to give it that unique RUFIO touch.

JP looked around the apartment for some inspiration. There was a baseball game on tv . . . Laura was watching baseball? That reminded him. He had toyed with an idea some weeks before. JP collected discarded baseball cards he found in the gutter. He was intrigued by the concept: photos on the front, statistics on the back. (His favorite, Tug McGraw's "Ya Gotta Believe!", he had pinned up on his bulletin board.) He would develop a series of package hangtags which, like baseball cards, could be collected by his customers. On one side would be a picture of JP. (He was beginning to view himself in third person, like a product. He would have to be careful.) On the other side, he would print quotes from himself on whatever he happened to be concerned about at the time. This would appeal to that human "cute," but most importantly, it would keep the lines of communication open between him and his brother and sister canines.

JP went to work. The first tag would have four different photographs of him wearing a different style t-shirt in each. On the back: a quote introducing himself and explaining why he had designed the t-shirts.

RUFIO*: Once free to run naked thru the countryside, I'm now an Urban Dog.

Sure I've had to make adjustments:
to the smell of exhaust instead of the scent of fresh cut grass;
to garbage instead of mulch;
to hydrants & tires instead of trees.

But the furs & jewels of some urban cousins are just not my thing . . .

So I've designed a line of T-SHIRTS for me & for you:

Dogs of Independent Spirit
Dogs of the '70's

RUFIO*

1.

RAISE CANINE CONSCIOUSNESS

KEEP NEW YORK CITY CLEAN

WALK IN THE STREETS...

Since I've been in the city I've learned not to use the sidewalks.
The only problem is I've also had to learn to walk with my head down so I don't step in the garbage humans throw into the streets...

(Sometimes I don't mind it too much -- one night I found a whole cheeseburger...)

2.

Wishing All My Friends
an International Canine Season's Greetings

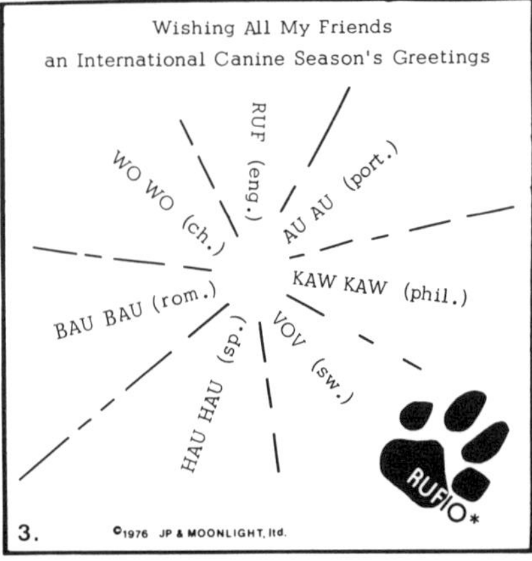

3.

The second tag would be a Christmas greeting. JP took some license with the classic multilingual United Nations "Peace on Earth" holiday card. For his version, JP collected barks in different languages. The hardest to come by was Chinese. He could find nothing in the library to help him. One day he got into a taxi to go uptown. It was his good luck that this cab driver was Chinese. JP did not hesitate. Without thinking to explain, he asked the cabbie to make the sound that dogs make in Chinese. The cabbie did not hesitate either: "Wo, Wo." Of course! Of course! JP added it to his already completed Swedish, Portuguese, Philippino, Spanish, Romanian and English research . . . RUF!

Tag #3 was special to JP. It marked the beginning of his role as activist philanthropist. It was his "Keep New York City Clean" tag.

To polish his product presentation JP took the baseball card concept one step further. He had business cards made up with pictures of himself on the back. There were five different poses. Was it ego or promotional genius? Whenever Laura offered someone her card, they would ask her for the full set . . . I'll trade you three "George Bretts" for one "JP RUFIO."

JP & MOONLIGHT, ltd.

proudly announces

the premiere collection of

RUFIO*s T-SHIRT ··· the CANINE CLASSIC*

for the canine whose consciousness is raised...

and wants clothing to reflect this life-style

THE TRADE SHOW CIRCUIT

Heads turned as he padded by. Exhibitors leaned out over their booths. Incredulous chuckles crossed their lips. Amused buyers, standing in the aisles, stepped aside to let him pass. Some began to follow him. They'd never seen anything like him: an Afro-haired French poodle in a t-shirt.

JP was making his first appearance at The National Association of the Pet Industry Trade Show. RUFIO's CANINE CLASSICs were being introduced to the trade. Ironically, JP had had to get special permission to attend: No Dogs Allowed. JP would think about reporting it to the ACLU after the show. For now he was not about to let anything stop him from enjoying his debut.

Assuming the role of a canine pied piper, he developed a routine to attract the buyers to his booth. Every hour or so, he would return to the booth, put on a different t-shirt and go back to wandering around the show. He told Laura it was for publicity, which it was. But JP had ulterior motives. He had discovered that some of the booths were selling food. He let his nose be his guide. He went with the smells. Because everyone thought he was so adorable he was getting free samples from everywhere. Within a few hours he was stuffed. The t-shirts were beginning to get tight.

Like a carnival shill, he would go out, circle the show and entice the unsuspecting customers to follow him back to his booth. Once back at the booth, they were shown his full ready-to-wear collection. JP wrote his first orders: Saks Fifth Avenue, B. Altman's, The Kennelworth Hotel for Dogs, East Hampton's Pets Painted with Love and more. He was in business.

* * *

The booth next to JP & MOONLIGHT's was empty. Sometime during the afternoon of the second day, a circle of people gathered on the floor, where the booth should have been. Laura looked over, thought it was strange, but shrugged her shoulders. After two days at a pet trade show, nothing fazed her.

Nothing except JP's sudden disappearance. She whistled for him. No JP. She called his name. He didn't come. All Laura could think of was the elevators leading to the lobby leading to the street. She panicked: JP lost out on the streets of New York! She might never see him again. JP, sold into puppy prostitution, becoming a bowery bum, or worse yet, a bag dog. No one was paying any attention to her trauma. More and more people had joined the group on the floor and were captivated by whatever beast was at their center. Whatever "beast?"

Laura moved in closer to get a better look. Desperately she peered into the center. It wasn't JP. The assembled group was mesmerized by a pair of ferrets on leashes. They were actually kind of cute. At another time Laura would have joined the circle. But now, where was The Kid? Laura stood still, trying to calm herself. Then she heard it.

JP, of late, had taken to wearing his chain collar with all his dog tags attached. He thought it was "Hollywood." Laura heard their soft clanging. But from where? She looked again at the circle. Very slowly she checked out every face staring in at the weasels. There were a couple of hairy faces, but on closer examination, they were all bearded humans. Laura's eyes examined clothing for anything unusual. Nothing. She checked the backsides of the participants. None of them looked familiar or interesting. Something caught her eye. She could not quite focus on it, it was moving too fast. She moved closer. Her eyes squinted as they followed the speeding object towards the middle of the circle. Her whole body sighed.

There he was. He had been there all the time. JP, squeezed into the gathering, was shoulder to shoulder with the "other" humans fascinated by the ferrets. No one had even noticed him. Laura hadn't been able to identify him because the man next to him was wearing a red and navy rugby t-shirt just like the one JP was wearing.

* * *

All of JP's adventures during this first trade show were not so quiet nor so harmless. Across the aisle from JP & MOONLIGHT's display was a booth selling rare birds and baby parrots. The baby parrots were just learning to talk. JP was fascinated with the smells and sounds from this group. Lucky for the birds, their cages were perched up high enough to be out of his reach. Oh, JP would never harm them, but when he is curious about something, he is compulsive about checking it out.

JP barked his frustration at not being able to make direct contact with the parrots. He barked Friday, he barked Saturday and he barked Sunday. Sunday afternoon as she started to take down the booth (the show was ending in an hour), Laura heard JP barking again. She snapped at him to be quiet, enough was enough. But JP was curled up on a chair, sleeping like an angel. Laura knew she had just heard him speak. No one else sounded like him. Confused, she looked around. Oh, no! She gasped her disbelief. Across the aisle, those exotic and expensive baby parrots were barking. Their mimic of JP was perfect. The owner was hysterically tearing her hair out: "I'll never be able to sell them. No one wants a parrot who barks." RUF!

* * *

JP jumped into the trade show circuit with all fours. With each show he learned a little more about his newly adopted profession. Orders for the t-shirts were coming in faster than the factory could turn them out. This was pretty heady stuff. JP strutted around telling other dogs that he deserved his success 'cause he had paid his dues. He was beginning to think he knew it all.

At one trade show two business students from Long Island University approached JP. They had questions about product development and marketing. JP told them to feel free, ask him anything.

"Well, Sir, what is JP & MOONLIGHT's distribution plan?" JP tilted his head coyly: What is a distribution plan? JP stopped strutting and went back to work.

* * *

As far as JP was concerned, the Gift Trade Show at the New York Coliseum was the most important human trade show of the year. It was almost impossible to get a booth unless you reserved years in advance or had a major sales representative organization take you in. JP was lucky. He found two groups to represent him. Each had very different clientele, so there was no conflict of interest. He was very pleased with the way things were working out.

But once again, Laura had to be the one to tell him: No Dogs Allowed. Two months before JP had

RUFIO*s T~SHIRT

Photograph by Chuck Serra

been barred from attending another human trade show, the Fashion Boutique Show. He had decided then not to make too much of it. But this time he had had it. Enough of this back-of-the-bus treatment. JP organized. He put out a call to his brothers and sisters to picket the Coliseum during the trade show. To encourage participation, JP promised a free t-shirt to every dog who showed up for the DOG-IN.

While JP peacefully led his band of hounds outside, Laura was overseeing the selling of RUFIO's T-Shirts inside. She was enjoying watching her salesmen do the work rather than having to do it herself.

They were all standing around joking and writing up orders when a seamy looking, white-haired man started circling the RUFIO display rack. One salesman nudged another. The mood changed. They stopped joking. Two of them moved protectively towards Laura who stood nearest the rack. "That's him. Move away." The man moved in closer to the shirts. The salesmen cautiously formed a circle around him. There was quiet tension. All eyes were on the white-haired gentleman who was now snaking toward the t-shirts.

Then like a shot he did it. His hand went up. He grabbed a shirt. He stuck it in his jacket. The salesmen moved just as swiftly. Their hands were in his jacket. The t-shirt was retrieved. The man shoved one of the salesmen trying to get the shirt back. The salesman fell on the floor. Another salesman jumped on the man. A third salesman with fist clenched moved in to join the fray. But the man screamed "Enough." He let go of the t-shirt package and rushed away. Laura couldn't believe what had just happened. She was sorry JP had missed all the action. He would be disappointed to learn that while he was dissenting peacefully there had been a real "hot" dogfight over his t-shirts.

A sixty year old cigar-chomping manufacturer trying to steal a dog t-shirt to copy it onto his line: a strange form of flattery but proof enough. RUFIO's CANINE CLASSICs were a success . . . RUF!

* * *

JP was too busy to fight every trade show organization which barred him from attending. He and Laura decided to create a fake RUFIO. They bought a stuffed animal, a white St. Bernard, dyed him black, added a wool yarn Afro, dressed him in a rugby shirt and put him to work.

At that time JP was featuring the rugby shirt in a Back-To-School Promotion. He had borrowed a pair of Laura's horn-rimmed glasses and some of her books for his promotional pictures. JP put the glasses on his double and sent him to represent him at the Mail Order Trade Show.

Laura worked the JP & MOONLIGHT booth by herself. She was quite bored. Most in attendance were not writing orders, just browsing. She could be using her time better back at the apartment.

A big bumbling man stopped in front of the booth to blow his nose. He halfwittedly looked over the booth. Then suddenly he slapped his side in disbelief. "There it is. I knew somebody was going to do it someday."

Laura smiled politely, "Would you like to see the whole line?"

Ignoring her, "I saw a dog in them out at Roosevelt Field Mall. I knew it wouldn't be too long. People will buy anything for their dogs. I knew it wouldn't be long."

Photograph by Chuck Serra

"Was the dog you saw wearing one of these t-shirts?"

"T-shirts? What are you talking about, t-shirts?" He blew his nose again. "I'm talking about the glasses." Pointing proudly to his head, "I knew when I saw that one dog wearing them, that all of them would start wearing glasses . . . " RUF!

"The dog has seldom been successful in pulling man up to its level of sagacity, but man has frequently dragged the dog down to his."

—James Thurber

JP was not allowed to attend the Westminster Kennel Club Dog Show. He was so disappointed. He even sent them his papers to prove that he had two champions in his lineage. (JP had never admitted to that before, it didn't fit his image.) But the papers didn't help, only dogs in competition could attend. It was just as well. For sure, JP would have had a heart attack if he had been there and seen poodles sauntering about in curlers and hair nets!

* * *

JP paid no attention to his or anyone else's breeding. He never judged other dogs, or people, by their papers. He took everyone at face value. His instincts generally served him well.

At one trade show, he met two bright women journalists who were doing research for a book. JP took to them. And very quickly he had them eating out of his paw, or so he thought.

They adored JP's Afro, his clothes and, of course, his free spirit. They seductively told JP how perfect he would be for their book: a self-made dog . . . a dog who padded to a different drummer. They made such a fuss over him. But then they said it: "Thank goodness you're not one of them."

One of them?

"A purebred."

Why, what's wrong with "them?"

"Oh nothing. But we won't have any of them in our book . . . only mongrels and mixed breeds."

JP's heart sank. He was shattered. He thought they had liked him for himself. Not because they thought he was something else. He was scared to tell them the truth. He had really liked them and he wanted them to like him. But he could not live a lie. He was who he was. He raised his head high. He was a purebred poodle.

The two women looked at each other embarrassed and stunned. "Oh, dear. Well that's all right."

"Yes," said the other. "Some of our best friends . . . we'll be in touch." They made a hasty retreat.

JP felt depressed and sour all day.

I CAN GET IT FOR YOU WHOLESALE

JP collected around him a diverse sales staff. He contracted sales representative showrooms in New York, Los Angeles and Dallas. Several professional salespeople carved out their own CANINE CLASSIC territories. And there were those who turned salesmen to make money from their friend JP's entrepreneurial journey into canine couture.

They sold to department stores (Saks Fifth Avenue, Bloomingdale's, Gimbels); pet shops (Teacher's Pet of Chester, New Jersey; Grooming Table of Dallas, Texas; La Tienda of Sanibel, Florida; Puppy Prince of Pennsylvania); gift shops (Mr. Bernard's of Bal Harbor, Florida); fashion shops (Lilly Pulitzer) and even drugstore chains (Belknap's Super Drugs, Missouri). Gift catalogues, such as "Joan Cook," "Kaleidescope" and "Stratford House," offered the t-shirts to their at-home shoppers.

RUFIO's CANINE CLASSIC was selling in twenty-eight states throughout the United States and in Japan. That's right, Japan. While the Japanese designers were taking over Seventh Avenue by storm, JP's collection was selling out in Takashimaya, Tokyo's most extraordinary department store.

TOSHISHO & CO., LTD.

Exporters - Manufacturers - Importers

Taisei Building—Office No. 611-612
No. 78, 6-chome, Sumiyoshi-cho,
Naka-ku, Yokohama, Japan

CABLE ADDRESS:
"YUTOSHI" YOKOHAMA
CODE USED:
BENTLEY'S 5TH
ACME
TEL: (651) 2714
(651) 1421

REF. NO.

YOKOHAMA,

JP & MOONLIGHT, LTD.
101 West 12th Street,
New York, N. Y., 10011
U. S. A.

Re: Dog T-Shirts:

Gentlemen:

We certainly received your catalogue, photos, price list, and other informations of your RUFIO*s CANINE CLASSIC* T-Shirt for Dogs sent to us by Air Mail postage.

We express our deep gratitude for your favor of having sent these to us as this to our request. We truly thank you very much for your kind managements at this time.

We are surprised at the excellent item of your T-Shirt for Dogs.

... making the sales activity to the
... le these.
... ese market,
... stigatio

UNIVERSAL TRADING CO., LTD.

EXPORTERS & MANUFACTURER'S AGENTS
P. O. BOX 80, ASAKUSA, TOKYO, JAPAN
TEL. 841 9687

CABLE ADDRESS:
"UNIVHORIE" TOKYO

BRANCH: OSAKA

JP & Moonlight, Ltd.
101 West 12 Street,
New York. 10011.

With reference to your T-shirts, we would like to know if you are making pet pants matching the dress so that we can sell them in combination.

Customers' inquiries are coming in along with this line one after another so if you could arrange for the samples we would appreciate it.

Hoping to hear from you soon,

Yours very truly,

UNIVERSAL TRADING CO., LTD.

JP learned fast that salesmen were a breed unto themselves. Some of them were real animals. All of them had to be handled . . .

JP padded into the conference room. He trotted to the head of the table and jumped up on the chair. He patiently waited for the others to join him. This important fashion store chain had wanted to meet the designer behind the RUFIO Collection before it committed itself to a major order. Although JP had not been called on to participate in many of these sales meetings, he handled himself with skill and decorum. He was fast becoming a dog of the world.

His sales representative, a big fat pompous man, sat down next to their host, a corporate merchandise buyer. The salesman all but ignored JP. He did not mind taking his commission money from him. He just disliked taking orders from a dog, no matter what his qualifications.

Nonetheless, the meeting proceeded smoothly. JP and the corporate buyer got on very well. The buyer had done his homework. He had found out about JP's penchant for cheese and had brought along several slices. He had the President of JP & MOONLIGHT, ltd. eating out of his hand. The 20% commission salesman did not like the way things were going.

JP and the company man were deep into their negotiations. The salesman had had enough. He took a bill out of his wallet, reached over and interrupted JP: "Here's $10.00, Kid. Go down to the lobby and get me some cigarettes."

The buyer looked disapprovingly at the salesman: "He's the President of your company!"

JP, not wanting to make waves at such an important meeting, showed uncommon restraint and took the money. He slid down from his chair and nosed his way to the door. But there he stopped. Thinking better of it, he turned around. In icy silence he scrutinized his employee. A low and dangerous growl filled the room. He drew himself up to his full height. With apologies to the gentleman buyer, JP spit out the money and lunged under the table. There with great panache, he chomped into his salesman's leg.

> **"The dog to gain some private ends,**
> **Went mad and bit the man . . .**
> **The man recovered of the bite.**
> **The dog it was that died."**
>
> **—Oliver Goldsmith,**
> **"The Vicar of Wakefield"**

It was at times like this that a good game of tennis was the only release. JP was a tennis freak. He had two court heroes: Vitas Geralitis and Guillermo Vilas. Vitas because he was New York like JP: fast talking, fast moving and bursting with energy; and Vilas because he was the poet, the reflection of JP's sensitive side. And most significantly, all three of them wore their hair the same way.

JP was a jock at heart. He loved all sports. He thrived on competition. So it was natural that for his own leisure he designed himself a satin basketball jacket, which he wore for football practice, a fishnet golf shirt and a "Devil Dog" metallic motorcycle jacket.

Basketball

Tennis

Golf

Motorcycling

"I would rather see a portrait of a dog that I know, than all the allegorical paintings they can show me in the world."

—Samuel Johnson

JP enjoyed very good business relationships with most of his stores. In addition to selling dog clothes, one of JP's favorite customers painted pets' portraits at her shop in East Hampton, New York. Lois was very gifted at what she did. But as hard a time as JP had had philosophically accepting the idea of clothing for dogs, he could not fathom hanging a pet's portrait. That was beyond his comprehension.

But the lady was very fond of JP and adored a NY Post photograph of him in his tuxedo. JP was such a sucker for flattery. He was not sure how it happened but she did sweet talk him into "letting" her do his portrait in exchange for two dozen RUFIO T-Shirts. Well, after all, she was one of his biggest fans.

JP did not say anything to Laura about it. He was sure she would just laugh at him. Besides, he probably wasn't going to like the painting enough to show her.

The portrait arrived. Lois had captured the best of JP: the gleam in his eye, the smile that always seemed ready to form on his lips, his hairy round belly and even the humor inside his head. JP was really embarrassed by the great pleasure he took in his own picture. He knew he had reached the cutting edge of selling out. But he didn't care. He loved his portrait. And he was proud of it.

Laura agreed. No denying it, the painting did have a certain "Je ne sais quoi." To dramatize its unique dignity, Laura surprised JP with a special plaque she had made just for his portrait:

JP RUFIO — CHAIRMAN OF THE BOARD.

NEW YORK POST

Eugenia Sheppard Around the Town

BLACK TIE OPTIONAL

Rufio has the perfect solution for the dog who has everything and asks the question, "What shall I wear on New Year's Eve?"

For all those parties that call for black tie, Rufio suggests a black-tie T-shirt from his latest ready-to-wear collection.

The group of shirts, which come in small, medium and large, are priced at around $7.50, and are available at Saks Fifth Avenue, B. Altman, Bloomingdale's and other stores.

Other doggie delights from the shirt collection, called Canine Classics, each labeled with Rufio's signature pawprint, include a Rugby stripe, a tie-dye and a do-it-yourself style with iron-on letters.

Rufio balks at taking all of the credit and admits having a little help from his friend and associate, **Laura Nadworny**, who understands his creative yearning to lead more than just a dog's life.

Post Photo by Terence McCarten

Rufio

"A Dog, more than any other creature, it seems to me, gets interested in one subject, theme, or object, in life, and pursues it with a fixity of purpose which would be inspiring to man if it weren't so troublesome."

—EB White
"One Man's Meat"

JP took to the media like a dog to a bone. He would have spent all his time creating publicity events if he could. Well, he couldn't. But he did stretch himself to his own limits to make the most of his successful situation.

The first journalist who captured his attention, and his heart, was Ms. Eugenia Sheppard of the New York Post. Reading in her society column about a visiting kangaroo dignitary from Australia, JP sent her his collection's debut announcement. Within days her office called, interviewed JP and sent a photographer out to take pictures. JP RUFIO made his newspaper debut, studded up in his tuxedo t-shirt on the society pages under the banner: "Black Tie Optional."

* * *

Arch Campbell, a reporter at WRC-TV, the Washington, DC NBC affiliate, picked up on JP's "Gift for the Dog who has Everything" press release. His report on this unique Christmas present for that "other" member of the family, was shown on NBC affiliates throughout the country including Phoenix, Nashville, Miami and Cleveland, Ohio. Orders started coming in from all over the nation . . .

* * *

JP's naturally competitive spirit held him in an adversary position with almost every dog he saw on television. He wanted that spotlight for himself. One dog receiving much attention at the time was a bulldog named Winston. JP was not envious of him. He liked Winston. He was a dog's dog.

Winston's human being was Dr. Frank Field, the weatherman on WNBC-TV in New York. Winston was fighting a losing battle against discrimination. He had been making regular appearances on the news show with Dr. Field. He was an instant celebrity. Fan mail poured into the station. The news program was now competing for ratings with Winston not WABC or WCBS. The news director, responding to some sense of journalistic responsibility, was concerned that the news show was losing its dignity and integrity. Humans, JP thought, should get their priorities straight. At last, millions of New Yorkers had a good reason to watch the news.

JP, in a gesture of brotherhood, sent Winston two t-shirts: the red & navy rugby and the tuxedo. For weeks JP heard nothing from him. Maybe bulldogs don't know how to write?

It was Christmas eve. JP flipped on the tv. It was a good thing he did. Dr. Field had just introduced Winston. He was on the program to show off his Christmas presents. There he was. Around his neck was a spiked collar to make any Hell's Angel jealous. And on his body, RUFIO's Rugby T-Shirt! Winston looked tough.

One week later, on New Year's Eve, anchorman Chuck Scarborough announced on the 6 o'clock news that Winston would join them at 11 o'clock to celebrate the holiday. He would be wearing his tuxedo t-shirt. JP pulled out all the stops, as well as all his rags, bones and toys. Looking at the scene in JP's house, one would have thought that JP was unaccustomed to publicity and triumph. Laura broke out the champagne and cheese.

Throughout the evening, Scarborough's face appeared on the screen to remind viewers to stay tuned to see Winston welcome in the New Year in his tuxedo. 11 o'clock came. There was Scarborough. There was Frank Field. But there was no Winston. JP nervously slurped up another bowl of champagne.

It was time for the weather. Field, standing in front of the weather map, informed the viewers that Winston would not be joining him. The news director had fired Winston. He was no longer a member of the news team. JP moved to turn off the tv.

"But for those of you who tuned in just to see Winston in his tuxedo . . . Here it is." JP froze in place. There was Dr. Frank Field, distinguished weatherman, standing in front of all the cameras and all of New York, New Jersey and Connecticut, holding up RUFIO's Tuxedo T-shirt. JP was howling. He could never afford that kind of publicity.

Dr. Field went on to tell his audience that they could send in for a free picture of Winston in his tuxedo. The story of Winston's tuxedo dismissal made headlines in New York Magazine, the Daily News, and The Miami Herald. JP hated to be making out on someone else's misfortune. He shared his thoughts with Winston the only way he knew how: he sent him the entire CANINE CLASSIC Ready-To-Wear Collection . . . RUF!

ONE DOLLAR DEC. 26, 1977/JAN. 2, 1978

Dan Dorfman on the 1978 Stock Market: "Watch Out!"

1977
The Year in Words and Pictures

The Bubbles Burst: Experts Rate the Status Champagnes

NEW YORK

"Arf," says Winston.
NBC's Frank Field admitted that his English bulldog, Winston, received more fan mail than he did following an appearance on the nightly news broadcast. One viewer sent Winston a tuxedo T-shirt. Despite the dog's good ratings, one NBC vice-president was not impressed. He sent down an order banning Winston from future appearances.

DAILY NEWS

Why Pooch Isn't Poring Over the News

Winston, an English Bull, Exiled by NBC

Why is that cloud following Frank Field? Why doesn't that cloud go away and stop raining on Frank's parade? How could anybody be so cold to such a warm guy?

"If this keeps up, I may wind up with Tex Antoine in the Bahamas," Field said yesterday as the icy exchange between himself and Joe Bartelme dropped the temperature to freez-

PETER COUTROS

ing over at NBC, where Frank nightly tells his audience what's in store in the weather.

Field's brouhaha with Bartelme, who is in charge of news programs on NBC-owned stations, has to do with Winston, an English bulldog whose name is derived from Winston Churchill, who also used to get into t he papers a lot.

"My son, Storm," brought the dog home a few months ago as a gift for my wife and myself," Field explained yesterday, one eye fixed on a cold weather front coming down from Anchorage and the other focused on some turbulence developing in Bartelme's office.

"He was just a pup, but he was more than we could accommodate at the apartment, so I decided to bring him in here, to my office," Field went on, adding that tending to the dog's toilet

Frank Field and Winston.

needs resolved the Field's problem of what to do with all those Sunday supplements piling up in the apartment.

One night, Tom Snyder, who anchors the Six O-Clock News with Chuck Scarborough, coaxed Winston into camera range and, pretty soon, the pooch became a regular of sorts on Field's weather segment.

Wednesday night, Scarborough told his viewers to tune in at 11 p.m. and catch Winston in the tux (a painted sweat shirt) he was going to wear on New Year's Eve.

That's when the snit hit the fan. Bartelme called Scarsborough and said that Winston would appear on the 11 o'clock show over his dead option renewal.

Bartelme's complaint was that things were getting too frivolous and that you had to draw the line somewhere, especially on a news program. Winston was the line. No matter what all those people out there in TV-land thought, Winston's career was over, as far as Bartelme was concerned.

Wednesday night, with millions waiting to catch Winston nibbling on Field's shoe laces, all Frank could show them was the sweatshirt-tux, minus Winston; which is like Sonny without Cher, Orlando without Dawn, Jimmy without Rosalynn.

Somebody said that a mangement type's telling a star how to run his show is like the tail wagging the dog. Somebody else said that Bartelme was barking up the wrong tree. Yet another suggested that NBC stood for No Bow-wows Considered.

THE PRODIGAL SON RETURNS

JP was dying to do a "Come Meet the Designer Day." All the big names in fashion did it. Why not him? It was arranged. The Gallimaufry, one of JP's favorite stores, in Croton, New York (near where he had grown up) would sponsor the day. JP was going home. He couldn't wait. The local press was notified.

The day arrived, sunny and warm. The headlines in the Citizen Register (a Gannett paper) shouted:

"PUTTING ON THE DOG WITH CASUAL CANINE FASHIONS

A Day in the Life . . ."

It was a real "hometown dog makes good" story. The day was an emotional and financial success. Who said you can't go home again?

Putting on the dog' with

By BETH SMITH

A Day in the Life...

Jeweled collars, velvet winter coats and boots are not Rufio's thing.

He's a T-shirt freak, an unusual hangup for a miniature poodle (usually so fussy about their dress) but not necessarily for dogdom in general. Rufio and his human buddy, Laura Nadworny, are on the road to success designing, modeling and marketing a new line of casual canine fashions.

Rufio, 12 years old but still swinging, spent most of his life frisking ungroomed and unclothed through the grassy environs of Briarcliff. When his owners, Laura's parents, moved out of the state, they asked Laura if he could live with her. She consented, and he moved to Manhattan. Laura and Rufio (his call name is J.P.) soon realized that four-footed creatures in the city simply cannot appear in public unclad. Small city dogs, especially miniature poodles, generally have wardrobes that would put Cher to shame. One chilly day, when Rufio was shivering from a close clip done at the grooming parlor, Laura bought a child's sweatshirt and put it on him.

RUFIO REBELLED at first, then realized that one cannot hold a mouthful of sleeve and walk at the same time without falling flat on one's face. He accepted it, Laura loved it, and Canine Classics was born.

Laura, a graduate of Parsons School of Design and New york University with a master's in broadcasting, has up to now earned her living designing clothes. She hopes to eventually write for television and film production, but at the moment has her hands full with her new company, J.P. and Moonlight, Ltd. She (and Rufio) are the company.

Laura has personally written the catch copy, the tags, designed the fashions, marketed them to stores in several states and conducted, with Rufio, an in-person and in-poodle advertising campaign. Last Sunday she and the well-dressed dog were guests for "Meet the Designer Day" at Marimekko at Gallimaufry in Croton.

There are seven different styles for sale. The Earth Shirt, which says EARTH on it, is a rust tie-dye shirt that can be worn with Earth Shoes while one is meditating, protesting, or raising one's consciousness. The JOG shirt is for the health and exercise nut. The striped red and blue rugby T-shirt is perfect for playing ball or going to summer camp, and for marriages and black tie affairs, Rufio provides a white tuxedo complete with red carnation and double lapel. Simple beige and black T-shirts come with letter kits so dog owners can personalize their pets' apparel. For those fast dashes after the neighbor's cat or just keeping toasty on cold winter days, Rufio has a red sweatshirt with cutoff sleeves. The flashy dresser will prefer Rufio's yellow and blue waterproof nylon Italian-style bicycle jacket.

LAURA SAID she designed the fashions as tongue-in-cheek gifts to people who have everything, including dogs. What she didn't expect was the huge reaction she has gotten from pet owners themselves.

Among the stores carrying Canine Classics are Choice Pets, Inc. at the Arcadian Shopping Center in Ossining, Abraham & Strauss, Bloomingdale's, B. Altman & Co., Saks Fifth Avenue, The Kennelworth, Gallimaufry in Croton, the Ark in Flemington, N.J., and Pets Painted With Love in Easthamp-

casual canine fashions

All the fashions carry Rufio's paw print, something like the Hang Ten footprints, and are sold in individual plastic bags with handles. Laura also has introduced a narrative on the tags which tells Rufio's story (from grass to class) and his philosophy about keeping New York clean by taking to the streets on occasion rather than the sidewalks.

ton. Stores in Philadelphia and even as far south as Tennessee have begun requesting the fashions.

Laura got the idea for the company one year ago, started it in April, then introduced the new line in September. The entire operation is being run from her apartment, with Rufio's supervision and occasional "rebarks."

All the fashions carry Rufio's paw print, something like the Hang Ten footprints, and are sold in individual plastic bags with handles. Laura has also introduced a narrative on the tags which tells Rufio's story (from grass to class) and his philosophy about keeping New York clean by taking to the streets on occasion rather than the sidewalks.

AFTER CHRISTMAS, Laura hopes to bring the business to nationwide distribution, and is even considering television advertising. She is learning about trademarks, screen printers, marketing, writing, and the million other skills that make or break a business. Her secret, she said, is that she never stops and asks herself what she is getting herself into. Her confidence and Rufio's sense of humor keep her going.

"Part of it is dumb luck," she said, "but I never thought I couldn't do it."

She does admit occasional regret that Rufio's fashions took off while some of her more brilliant ideas never made it. This crazy success could make her a millionaire or, as she predicts, "a madwoman."

Does Rufio ever mind his new role as a fashion-conscious trendsetter?

"Give him a piece of cheese and he'll do anything," Laura laughs. Somewhere around the fifth clothing change during a modeling session a bit of skim milk cheese smooths the temperamental star's ruff.

P.S. This reporter broke down and bought the rugby shirt for the very classy, cool, expensive, champion-sired German Shepherd she co-owns. Know why Hutch loves it? Because even the classiest dogs love to be downright silly once in a while!

BETH SMITH is Lifestyles Editor at the Citizen Register of Ossning.

"Give the dog an ill name and hang him."
—George Colman the Elder

JP was mellowing, sort of. He understood that with the extensive press coverage he was receiving, mistakes could happen. Because there were so many well known fashion designers, occasionally credit is given to the wrong person. JP was a victim of just such mistaken identity. He remembered a time when he would have ripped into that kind of sloppy reporting like so many rags.

A reporter with New York's afternoon paper interviewed a successful pet shop owner about the dog clothes she carried. The shopkeeper told the reporter that her line of t-shirts, including a JOG shirt were by RUFIO for Laura. The paper carried the story of "Ralph Lauren's jogging suit for dogs."

JP sent off a letter to the newspaper requesting an immediate correction. Only too aware of the prejudice in the fashion industry against dog designers, he was sure Mr. Lauren, whom he respected, would not be pleased with such a mistake. Besides, he, JP, also had a reputation to protect . . . RUF! RUF!

FOR IMMEDIATE RELEASE:

FASHION WARS !!!

Pits Canine Designer Against the Pack

Dogs do not live by Cheap Polyester alone.

Photograph by Jamison

There is only one RUFIO®s CANINE CLASSIC®

At Gift and Pet Stores Everywhere.

IN SICKNESS AND IN . . . TRAVEL

How long had she been sitting there? What time was it? She turned to the person on her right. He was an English sheepdog. He had a bandage around his leg, no watch. The Shih tzu leaning into her on her left was snoring. She was surrounded by rows and rows of benches, filled with dogs and cats, some sniffing, some dozing, some licking, others scratching themselves, all waiting their turn. She felt very uncomfortable in their midst. Except for JP, she had always preferred the company of humans.

She spotted a clock on the far wall. One o'clock in the morning? JP had called her at about 9 PM. Laura was out at a meeting and he wasn't feeling well. He didn't know what was wrong. Would she mind going with him up to the Animal Medical Center? She did not hesitate.

JP and the Doctor walked out of the examining room. JP had checked out fine. He was just dog tired. He needed a vacation. JP took one look at her. She had been sitting there so long, she looked like she needed a veterinarian. He handed her his leash and took her home. JP had such good friends.

* * *

The busier JP became the more travelling he was required to do. Public appearances, visits to stores, and meetings with buyers were his responsibility. He occasionally used the New York subway system to get around. It was real cheap for him. He was so short he just walked under the turnstiles. (A German shepherd transit cop stopped him once. But he was no match for JP. The next time JP saw him, he was wearing one of

JP's t-shirts.) But for the most part JP didn't like to use the subways. Their condition wasn't fit for a dog . . . RUF!

* * *

New York City taxis were another story. They were always a source of surprise and wonderment for JP . . .

One cabbie shared a secret with this Afro-haired captain of industry: the saga of his pet fish. Captured out of a Central Park pond, one summer long ago, this ten inch goldfish had lived with the cabbie for six years. They had a special friendship. But he, the fish, was getting old.

Whenever the cabbie returned home after a long hard day in the potholes of New York, he would be greeted by a happy fish. His entrance into their apartment would send the fish into bubbling circles around his bowl. The cabbie would jiggle his house keys and the fish would circle with delight. Because, the cabbie assured JP, the fish had exceptional hearing ability.

But alas, the years passed and things changed. The cabbie floundered over his words. It was so hard to talk about. His fish was going deaf.

No longer did he swimmingly greet him. In fact, often times the cabbie had to walk right up to the bowl and tap on its glass before the fish knew he was home. And sometimes, the fish did not even hear that.

JP was very touched by the cabbie's plight. But he didn't know what to say to him. He had never known anyone with a deaf fish.

* * *

When Laura told JP he was going to fly to Miami on business, JP couldn't wait. He took out his treasured 'Snoopy Fights the Red Baron' silk scarf, swept it around his neck in his most swashbuckling manner, put on his silver flight jacket (two minutes before it had been a sample bike jacket for RUFIO's next line) and with reminiscences of his most amazing flying dreams aloft in his head, JP was ready to go off into the wild blue yonder.

But this trip brought him swiftly back to earth. This flight demanded strict adherence to rules, not one of JP's favorite things, especially not when one of those rules meant packaging him for placement UNDER the seat. How humiliating!

Laura tried to accommodate the Chairman's needs by making a box more suited to him than those available for sale. She rehearsed JP getting in and out of it. She even decorated it with his favorite rags. He did not like it at all.

The veterinarian prescribed Valium for JP: 2.5 milligrams an hour before the flight and then again upon boarding. That would have knocked Laura for a loop.

She had it all figured out. JP, being sufficiently zonked when they boarded, would quietly slip under the seat in his box. After she settled into the flight, she would sneak him out of the box, onto her lap, where he would sleep like a puppy the whole way into Miami . . . a piece of cake.

Ha! Laura wrapped the pill in some cheese. JP spit out the pill and ate the cheese. She wrapped the pill in another piece of cheese. JP spit it out again. They tried this routine three more times. Desperate times demand desperate measures. Laura shoved the pill down her loved one's throat. How could she humiliate him like that? JP barked at her for fifteen minutes, nonstop. The airlines personnel and other passengers in the waiting room were eyeing them. JP drank some water and began to calm down.

It was time to board the plane. Laura blanketed another pill in the cheese. JP snapped it up—surprise. He begrudgingly got into the box. He hoped no one was watching. Laura took a deep breath and put the top on. JP went bananas.

He bounded out of the box. He jumped up and down on the chairs and passengers around him. He rolled over and over and over. How could Laura do this to him? How could she expect someone in his position (a self-made dog, Chairman of the Board, Philanthropist) to travel in a cardboard box. He was dancing as fast as he could.

A flight attendant came over to warn them that if JP did not quiet down and stay in the box, the pilot would not let him board. Laura realized the valium would have been better used if she had taken it.

Somehow, JP was in the box with the cover on. Not convinced by his momentary cooperation, Laura continued to whisper sweet nothings into the cardboard carton. She waited to be the last to board the plane. One of the other passengers, witnessing her dilemma, came over to offer his assistance. Michael also introduced himself to the box. He had a plan.

Laura stood up and held the box at waist height. Michael positioned himself exactly behind her, creating a two-headed, four-legged and four-armed monster. Michael slipped his arms around Laura's waist and took the box from her. Her arms were now free to hold the top of the box closed. This strange and intimate partnership walked as one onto the plane. The box barked so much, one astute passenger asked if there was a cat in there?

Michael settled Laura into her seat. His act of gallantry completed, he disappeared. JP did not "settle" in at all.

Laura cautiously removed the top of the box. For most of the flight, she sat doubled over, leaning down to scratch the Chairman's belly, to soothe his frayed nerves. (It was she who needed the tummy rub.) Slowly, slowly the motion of the plane lulled JP to sleep. Laura sat back to relax.

The flight attendants rolled the trays of food up the aisle. The smell of airline cuisine wafted through the cabin. JP's nose began to twitch. His eyes blinked open. His head tilted up. His tongue was hanging out. Food. JP was up and talking. Laura was doubled over once again. Miami could not arrive soon enough . . . RUF!

* * *

Laura walked into the Dade Animal Hospital. Her shoulders were stooped. There was a lump in her throat and deep circles under her eyes. She had not slept all night. The flowers in her hand were limp from being wrung. JP had gotten sick in the middle of the night. Laura had rushed him to this unfamiliar hospital away from home. She didn't know anything about it or its doctors. She was a wreck.

The veterinarian clogged out to the waiting room and motioned for her to follow him down a long antiseptic hallway. He didn't speak but his manner was soothing. The doctor led her to a vast open room and pointed her toward the far end.

JP was in a ward with a private cage. Laura rushed to him. He was just lying there. An intravenous tube was stuck in his arm. His EKG chart was pinned to the cage wall. Laura shoved the flowers, one at a time, through the wire openings of the cage. He looked up at her. He struggled to move closer to her. He was hurting. She crushed her face against the cage wiring so they were nose to nose. JP licked away Laura's tears. He laid back down and went to sleep.

The doctor came to get her. He gently explained that JP had collapsed, that he was in bad shape. He had just pushed himself too hard. If he did not slow down the next time could be fatal. His body was warning him.

Laura was crying. JP would never slow down. He was a workaholic. The vet tried to comfort her. JP was tough. He would pull through. The doctor would see to it. And he did. This doctor would always be one of Laura's favorites, he saved JP's life.

* * *

Like any other hyper-active entrepreneur, JP was limited in his ability to sit still for too long a recuperative period. He did, however, agree to check into a Miami dog spa for a couple of weeks for some R&R. Besides, it would give him a chance to cop some rays in his newly designed red & white stretch terrycloth tank top. Laura went back to New York by herself to take care of business. JP would fly back on his own.

This time JP decided to travel in the luggage department rather than in the cabin. He had heard some horror stories about dogs freezing to death, getting crushed to death or being abandoned to travel the world in the belly of a plane. It was all preferable to

Photograph by Chuck Serra

chancing a repeat of his last trip. Besides, he had it all figured out.

He bought himself a kennel carrier large enough to suit a travelling Labrador retriever. He then outfitted it with his best rags, some new rawhide bones and a dripless water bowl. He booked passage, paid a visit to a local groomer (who wasn't as wonderful as Jim & David of Caniche, but who was?). There's nothing like a good shampoo to make a mad dog feel better. Then he had JC (he was now on first name basis with his vet) give him a tranquilizing shot and pack him onto the plane.

At the Eastern Airlines Cargo Hanger at LaGuardia Airport, Laura paced anxiously. She had heard those horror stories too. Cargo luggage was the last to be unloaded. It was 20°F. Was JP sitting out there somewhere in the darkness of the runway, abandoned and freezing to death? Was he dressed properly?

At last, he arrived in his oversized kennel, freshly groomed, wearing his bright red fleece sweatshirt. He looked beautiful. He was alive.

Laura studied him a little more closely. His eyes were glazed, his pupils dilating, his head nodding. Two policemen came over to admire him, "Hey, what's the matter with your dog?"

"He's stoned. Oh, dear. You aren't going to arrest him, are you officer?" Laura mocked.

The two policemen laughed incredulously: "That's all we need: to have to start busting junkie dogs." RUF!

* * *

From the very first time JP was examined by Dr. K., it was another one of JP's adversary relationships. One of the doctor's assistants had startled JP by grabbing him by the nape of the neck. Naturally, JP defended himself: he snapped at her. But the doctor did not see the "grab" he only saw the "snap." JP never lived down this false image of ferocity . . .

It happened again. JP collapsed. For twenty-four hours he could not walk. He would not eat. The doctor told Laura not to move him. Laura was terrified. It looked grim. She insisted on bringing him to the vet's office.

The doctor examined him. JP was not moving. Despairing, Laura placed him down on the floor to see what he would do. She was afraid to let JP go. She was mumbling and crying.

All eyes were on JP, afraid he would painfully fall on his face. Wobbly legged, he stood up. He began to walk across the room, slowly at first and then with increased speed. He stumbled his way from one room to the next to the third. Laura was relieved, amused and embarrassed all at the same time.

Laura, the doctor and two assistants followed JP through a maze of hospital rooms. They couldn't find him. Dr. K. did not voice his worst fear that JP may have collapsed again (he was a very sick dog) and they might find him too late. Laura spotted him in a corner.

He was still standing. But what was he doing? None of them believed what they were seeing. JP, practically on his death bed, had discovered a bowl of cat food and was feasting away.

Frightened and finally convinced that he was only canine, JP put aside his orneriness long enough to listen to Dr. K. (for whom he had profound respect). He rested up and earned a perfect bill of health. With new insights into the meaning of life, JP was soon back on the job.

A DOG HOUSE OF HIS VERY OWN

JP padded into the office, briefcase in mouth. The executives in the offices he passed, waved absent-minded but friendly good mornings to him. It hadn't always been like that.

When Accountant #1 first suggested that it was time for JP & MOONLIGHT, ltd. to have its own offices, JP was of two minds. He knew how important an office was for "the image" of the company and JP was all for image building. However, it was money which could be better spent on product development and more targeted promotion. There were, after all, dogs out there who still did not know about RUFIO's T-Shirts (at least that's what the demographics were showing).

But Accountant #1 persisted, even coming up with an office for rent from another one of his clients. The price was right: JP would not have to put his pawprint on the dotted line, just a paw shake would do. "Shake." JP and Laura moved uptown to their new Madison Avenue corporate headquarters.

These days, JP always dressed for business. The Chairman of the Board could not walk around naked. Success had its drawbacks. But he adjusted. The first week in his new surroundings, everyone on the staff of the company he was renting from, found their way into his office to get a peek at him. Adulation is one thing, but curiosity is an invasion of privacy. Eventually, they did get used to him and he to them. In fact JP got so blasē, that if he was busy gnawing on his bone, he did not even take the time to look up when they stopped by. He was learning to play the management game.

DOGS ARE PEOPLE, TOO

JP's trips to his stores had convinced him of the need to provide his customers with a t-shirt display unit. While JP had been recuperating, Laura had begun the search for such a manufacturer. Now that he was back on the job, JP was in a hurry to finalize a deal, to get the racks made.

The receptionist announced the arrival of yet another display rack salesman. JP followed Laura out to greet him. He was getting impatient with this whole process. Laura said, "Hello." Then gesturing toward JP introduced him to the salesman: "This is JP RUFIO, my boss."

The salesman did a double take at Laura, to convince himself she was joking. Laura was very businesslike. She immediately launched into questions pertaining to the display racks. The salesman looked back and forth between the woman and the t-shirted dog. He was uneasy as he followed them back to their office.

He sat down on the sofa, opened his briefcase and took out his sample book. JP jumped up on the sofa, sat down next to him, and leaned over to sniff the book. Laura took out the sketches of the display rack JP wanted. The man reached over to take the sketches from Laura. JP also reached out, to the man's hand, and pulled it back to his, JP's, belly. Laura smiled, "I guess he likes you."

The salesman was now looking for the way out. He was getting very nervous. Laura was beginning to get irritated with his jumpiness. "What's the matter?"

"Can I just ask you one question?" he blurted out.

"What is your product?"

Laura looked at him and then at JP, coyly sitting next to him, and started laughing.

"Lady, are you crazy? What is so funny?"

There was this poor man, sitting next to a dog in a t-shirt that said "Dogs are People, too," talking to a woman who kept referring to that dog as her boss, and he had not been told what the product was . . .

RETURN OF THE MOTHER TRUCKERS

JP did not keep this office for very long. The President of the company renting to them decided he wanted to rent them a different space. So, he had JP moved. JP had to redesign their showroom headquarters: time which could have been better spent on business matters. Because their new space was larger and brighter, he decided not to argue the point.

They had been in this new office for just two months when Insurance Man #1 paid them a visit. He also worked with Accountant #1. He informed JP that the renting company's insurance would not cover JP & MOONLIGHT's merchandise and, therefore, JP had to move out.

Accountant #1 and the landlord shrugged their collective shoulders, "Sorry." JP went to the rag. The movers were hired for the second time in three months to move them back to 12th Street. JP had misunderstood. He had been under the impression that accountants were there to help their clients make money? RUF!

JP adjusted quickly to being back in the apartment. He had to. The display racks were coming: fifty 12x12x24 boxes.

For twenty minutes after their arrival, Laura could not reach JP. He had decided to get out from underfoot and had nested himself comfortably at the far end of the apartment with a good bone. The fifty boxes, which took up more than half of the one room studio, were piled up in front of him. JP was trapped. Laura threw pieces of cheese to him over the cardboard fortress, to keep him calm as she rearranged the boxes. There was only one solution to this overcrowding: sell the racks fast.

A new promotion was designed: one free display rack with every three dozen t-shirt order.

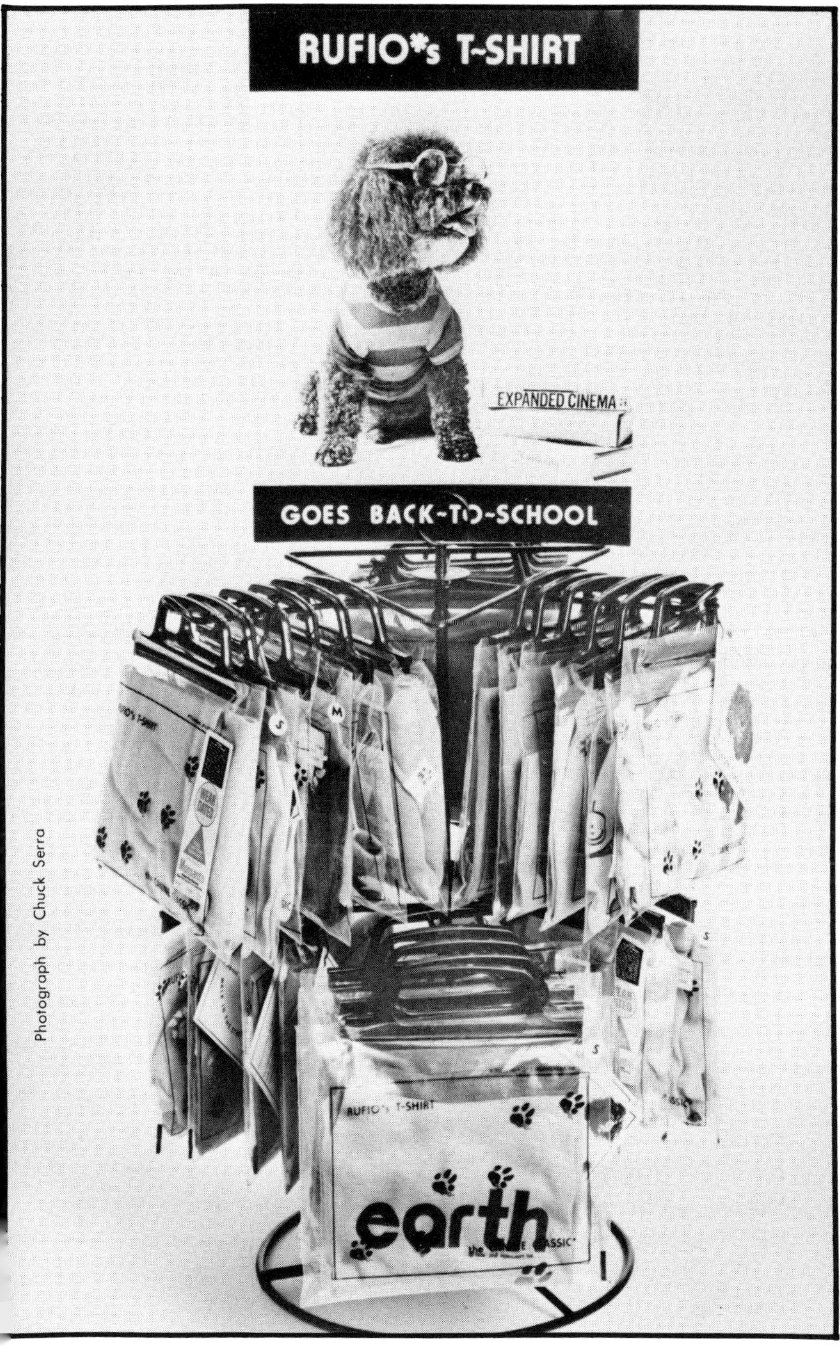

RUFIO*s T-SHIRT
EXPANDED CINEMA
GOES BACK-TO-SCHOOL
RUFIO's T-SHIRT
earth

Photograph by Chuck Serra

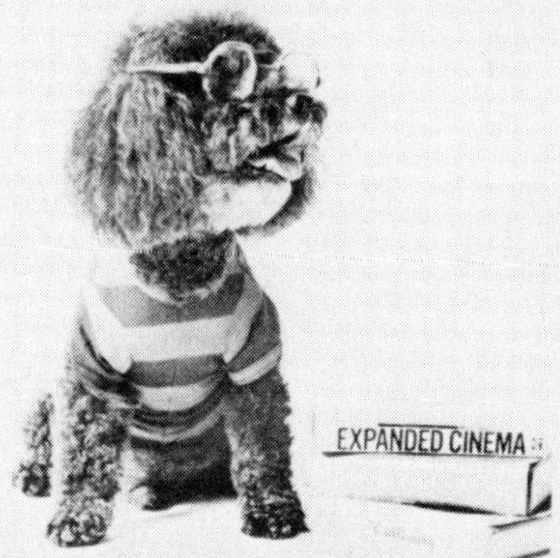

PACKING & . . .

JP knew that what he needed was a Soho loft, not a Village studio, but he had no time to go out and look for one. In fact he had very little time for anything. He was working doggedly to keep up with the orders which were now rolling in.

Finding workers to fold and package the finished shirts was a major priority of JP's. He demanded that the shirts be folded neatly; that the correct hangtag be attached to the right bag; that the bags never have a pawed over look. Quality control in this aspect of production was proving almost impossible.

The Pennsylvania factory did try to do the packaging but with disastrous results. Shirts were stuffed into the bags so violently that the bags ripped apart. JP, disturbed at the lack of pride the factory workers took in their work, was at his wit's end. He was being pushed to the wall. He did the only thing a conscientious manufacturer could do under such circumstances: he set up a sweatshop.

The first group of unskilled non-union workers JP hired were an eight year old, a ten year old and a twelve year old. He liked them: they were all short. But their hands had not developed the dexterity needed to handle this precise job. JP was relieved when their family took them away on vacation so he did not have to fire them.

The fourteen year old recruits who replaced them were a nightmare. They didn't last a week. JP was really down about this packaging problem. It was taking his time away from everything else. He had taken to compulsively eating dog biscuits. There had to be a better solution.

Suddenly, there they were: "the actresses," a group of New York University drama students. They were always "on." They loved to be the center of attention. JP was the perfect match for them. He appreciated their need to express themselves, although at times, even he thought they overdid it. But for awhile it was heaven. They folded, sang, soliloquyed, packaged, danced and, to Laura's great relief, walked JP for his relief.

But because the play was their thing, they were fickle to the Chairman. An audition, a reading, a show, or a party where they could be seen took priority. They just would never believe their future was in dog clothes.

After spending evening upon evening folding and packaging, JP resolved his problems. He had heard that, for a fraction of the cost of what union workers charged, the Federation for the Handicapped accepted industrial assignments. JP decided this would be a wonderful arrangement. It not only fulfilled his altruistic needs to serve his fellow being, it satisfied his newly acquired capitalistic drive to cut costs and save money. RUF!

. . . SHIPPING

JP slammed down the phone, put his sweatshirt on over his striped t-shirt (he was into the layered look), wrapped one of Laura's short wool scarves around his neck and padded out the door.

It was noon, Christmas eve. Out on the street beings were happily scurrying about overloaded with packages. It was beginning to snow. JP was on his way to Eighth Avenue, to the Port Authority Bus Terminal. This was pre-reconstruction days and the Port Authority was the seediest terminal in town.

The Pennsylvania factory had done it again. Three weeks before, in the middle of JP's busiest season, the manager of the factory had gone skydiving and broken both his arms and legs. No one else at the factory knew what to do with JP's order. After much barking and growling, JP and the new supervisor had gotten it straightened out and the last shipment was promised before the shipping lines closed for their two week holiday vacation.

The truckers had gone out on holiday three days ago. The shirts had finally been shipped this morning. They were on their way into Port Authority by Greyhound.

Before JP left the house, the factory had called to tell him what time the bus had left Pennsylvania and what time it would arrive in New York. JP trotted through the despair and filth of Port Authority until he found the expectant bus platform.

The bus had been scheduled to arrive at 1 PM. It was now three. JP was very uncomfortable padding back and forth. There were some real animals in these lower depths. He made friends with the bus drivers who

Photograph by Chuck Serra

were waiting around. They protected him. As one driver got ready to drive out, he would introduce JP to another driver. This continued throughout JP's vigil. They were good dog guards.

It was 7 PM. JP had called the factory, which swore it had put the shirts on the bus. He had called Wilkes-Barre, Pennsylvania: yes they had put package #8745 on the bus. He padded back and forth, back and forth.

The box arrived. JP grabbed a Red Cap by the pant leg and had him put him in a cab. It was 11:30 PM.

JP had never been so happy to be home. He felt so dirty he even allowed Laura to give him a bath. The last time she had tried to bathe JP was also the first time. She had carefully placed him in the tub as it filled with running water. He sat there for one rigid moment. Then, as if by levitation (JP was into that), he rose four feet above the tub and was out at a run, dripping bubbles as he went. Tonight there was no fight.

The next morning they opened the box. The factory had not bothered to mention in any of the dozen or so phone calls the day before, that they were shipping only half the order. Merry Christmas.

There were more exasperating conversations with the factory, leading to another holiday visit to Port Authority. This time the same twelve hour vigil was topped with a wino's toast to the New Year. JP was beginning to feel right at home . . . RUF!

"If God had meant for our minds to be stimulated, He wouldn't have given us television."

—Anonymous

The word was out. A local television talk show host wanted to see JP. He wanted to book JP for a guest appearance.

Dressed in his most convincingly fetching t-shirt "I Love My Human Being," JP made his way up 42nd Street to the tv production office. As he maneuvered his way through the legs of pimps, hookers, welfare mothers, johns, runaway kids, junkies and porno stars, he couldn't help but wonder if this was really the road to success.

The lobby smelled like a giant fire hydrant. The elevator doors opened and JP padded out. He opened the office door nose first and was greeted by the smell of stale cigars. The office was piles of autographed celebrity photos, yellowing issues of Variety, The Hollywood Reporter and too much abused furniture. JP barked to announce his arrival.

The tv personality didn't come out but yelled: "How are you doing JP? Be right with you. Hey, Pops, take my friend JP to the office down the hall."

A toothless, disheveled old man got up from behind the Varietys and opened the door for JP: "Walk this way."

The hallway looked like the building was in the process of being renovated. The "office down the hall" looked like it had been condemned. There were only three chairs. One had only three legs. Cigarette butts overflowed from beer cans turned ashtrays. JP's nose began to twitch. He was surrounded by half eaten, day old cheeseburgers. He went for it. A more intense sniff and JP, for the first time in his life, turned down cheese. It was green.

Pops was very solicitous of the Chairman. He took out a well used handkerchief and chivalrously wiped off a chair for him to jump up on. Pops sat down, too.

They just stared at each other. JP looked around and wondered to himself if this was what was meant by the expression "going to the dogs?" Pops began mumbling, something about the talk show host saying what a fine product JP had created. JP tilted his head appreciatively.

"I had an idea, once," Pops confided. "No one would listen to me. I still think it could have been a best seller."

JP's head tilted left. Pops leaned in to JP confidentially (JP wondered if this old man knew JP was a dog): "I wanted to publish the Bible in every language on earth." JP waited to hear more. There was no more.

Back in the real office, JP had a satisfactory visit with the New York tv personality. A tentative date was set for JP's guest appearance. JP liked this short man.

As JP was leaving the office, a chubby, sloppy looking blonde woman stopped him. She said she was the talk show host's publicity manager. She said, if JP was interested, she could get him some work in commercials. All he had to do was supply her with photographs and $50.00 for her initial efforts. After that she would work on commission. With JP's love for the spotlight, he was an easy mark.

JP never saw his $50.00 again. He never heard from the fat blond. She ripped him off . . . So much for doing business on 42nd Street . . . RUF!

* * *

JP watched tv whenever he had the time. He was trying to figure out what was meant by "programming in the public interest." As far as JP could tell, the only thing on the tube which seemed to satisfy that promise was the commercial for Kraft's single slices of American cheese.

"The Dog is the only animal who has seen his God."
—Anonymous

JP, his hair prematurely greying, his beard now snow white, was gracefully maturing into his leadership role. He brought with him the lessons of his youth. The activism, occult exploration and introspection he had indulged in in the 60's were a solid foundation on which to build his entrepreneurial dreams for the 80's. By integrating these forces into his lifestyle, he provided himself with balance, perspective and the most basic survival skill of all: humor. The altruism of the public JP RUFIO was the obvious result of such influences. His private life reflected much more.

* * *

His gaze was hypnotically drawn to the man next to him in the elevator. JP saw flowers and sunshine whenever he spoke. "He" was an Indian graduate student from New Delhi who lived in JP's apartment building. JP had a million questions to ask him but each time they met, JP became concerned that his questions might offend. After all there were some Eastern cultures who ate dogs and others who worshipped them. And JP could never remember which was which.

This time JP took a chance. The question which had been gnawing away at him had to do with reincarnation and the evolutionary path. He wanted to understand his place in the order of things. JP could get very serious. He was doing a man's job, with a woman's intelligence and instinct, but he was only a dog. He squatted up straight and begged for the man's attention. JP had not to say a word.

His teacher spoke, and JP heard George Harrison music in the background: "True the dog is lower in the evolutionary path than humans but yours is an old soul. You are moving to the universal center, toward eternal life. You are beyond us all."

JP had found his Guru. And he served JP well, especially in those times when the pressures of business got to be too much. Meditation was a wonderful thing . . . RUF!

* * *

With his tough little body alert, his eyes fixed upward, JP sat mesmerized by a wall in a darkened room.

It was 11 PM. Laura was just returning from a party. She and JP were visiting friends in Boston. They were staying in a convoluted railroad flat-type apartment. As she entered the apartment, she heard JP's barking mantra in the distance. She followed the sound through the darkness.

She turned on the light. There was JP making contact with a poster tacked to the wall in front of him. The poster was only color: grey with a splash of shocking pink. JP was unaware of Laura's presence. Spooked by this scene, Laura grabbed up her puppy and carried him back to the kitchen.

She sat him on a chair while she made some tea to calm herself. With her back to him, she kept up a nervous chatter. The kettle whistled. She poured the water and sat down. JP was gone.

Then it started again: JP was barking. She followed it back through the darkened rooms. He was poised at the foot of the same wall, staring up at the same pink-streaked poster.

Three more times, JP ritualistically returned. Each time Laura retrieved him. Finally, in desperation, she pulled down the poster and destroyed it. JP never again returned to that room. And he never explained himself . . .

STREET SMARTS

JP's street smarts and firm grip on reality aided in his fight against crime in the Naked City.

It was an early fall afternoon. JP handed Laura his leash and dragged her out to bask in the autumn sun. Perched on his hind legs, he pounced into her arms so that he could get closer to those warming rays.

But someone lurked in the shadows. A huge, grizzly man was circling them alcoholically. JP, peering over Laura's shoulder, spotted the predator weaving toward them. He began to growl. Laura looked in the direction of JP's irritation. She stiffened but did not move. The man took a step toward them. JP's growl turned into a teeth-baring snarl. The 300 pound predator froze in his place.

Fearlessly JP snapped at the intruder. Laura clung tightly to him. He was ready to attack. JP snarled again. The man suddenly and swiftly retreated. JP and Laura rushed back indoors. As Laura turned to be sure that they had not been followed, she saw two policemen chase and apprehend the awful man. Minutes before, the policemen told her that that same man had attacked and mugged a woman alone.

Laura hugged her ferocious twenty pound hero. JP's tail was speeding. He wasn't about to spoil this moment by telling Laura that when someone is afraid of dogs, it doesn't matter what size we are—we all look alike . . . RUF!

* * *

From the street, seventeen floors below, Laura heard a familiar sound. It was 7 o'clock in the morning. Groggy with sleep, she opened the blinds and craned her neck out the window to see what was going on. There was a picket line of maintenance workers marching in front of the building. They had been there yesterday. But that sound?

She turned back into the apartment to find JP. He was not there. She heard the sound again. It was so familiar. She took another look out the window. This time she saw what it was. It was JP. He was at it again.

He was down there, with a Local #32B placard tied to his back. To show solidarity with the workers, JP was out picketing his own building. A Dog of the People!

RAISING CANINE CONSCIOUSNESS

As JP's business acumen grew, so did his generosity. He made donations to Friends of Animals; Greenpeace and The World Wildlife Foundation. But it was the Humane Society of New York which received JP's special attentions.

His association with the Humane Society began simply enough. He had, much to his annoyance, an ever-growing pile of improperly sewn t-shirts. Some he was able to have the factory resew. But others, although wearable, he could never in good faith offer for sale.

Through his street connections, JP heard about the Humane Society's Adopt-a-Pet program. He liked the concept so much he donated those t-shirts to the Society to be given away with each adopted pet. He was on the road to philanthropy.

He was so turned on by the idea of helping his fellow canine, that he volunteered to write a column for the Humane Society Newsletter. He called it: "RAISING CANINE CONSCIOUSNESS WITH JP RUFIO." In it, he discussed issues of the day relevant to the canine population.

It was a big day for JP. In recognition of his good works, the Humane Society was anointing him their Spokesdog. This honor was to be bestowed upon him at ceremonies celebrating New York City's "Kindness to Animals" Week. Because it was a city function, JP had to share his spotlight with then New York City Mayor, Abraham Beame. But JP didn't mind. He liked this politician . . . He was short, like JP.

JP's moment arrived. He insisted Laura join him on the podium. The President of the Humane Society congratulated JP, shook his paw and then asked him to say a few words.

JP, who had been barking impatiently for the last hour as he waited his turn, was now silent. And so was his audience. They were waiting for JP to speak. JP looked at Laura, tilted his head coyly and waited with the rest of the audience. Laura found herself explaining to them that JP had a bad cold and had asked her to speak for him. She looked to the audience for some confirmation that they knew she was joking. She was met with only waves of sympathy for the Chairman. Laura spoke extemporaneously for fifteen minutes.

RAISING CANINE CONSCIOUSNESS WITH JP RUFIO

Humane Society BiAnnual Newsletter

My name is JP RUFIO, I'm a mini-poodle, philosopher and clothes designer. Every once in a while, I'll be expressing my opinions on issues that effect all of us Urban Animals here in the Humane Society of New York's Newsletter.

I haven't always been an Urban Canine and perhaps that gives me a unique insight into our problems and pleasures.

Once free to laze naked in the sunny countryside, I had to get used to the smell of exhaust instead of the scent of fresh cut lawns and being connected to a leash rather than running free . . .

But of all the adjustments I've had to make, the leash seems the most important. In a city filled with all kinds of sounds and smells that are bigger than me and which lead me by my nose and ears in five directions at once, the leash is my connection with my pet human being. She knows her way around these strange streets and odd vehicles and that leash is one way she tells me how much she loves me.

- A leash keeps me from running out in the street filled with cars that don't care
- When walking in the streets, a leash keeps me connected to my human who stands on 2 feet and can be seen by drivers, even when they can't see me
- A leash tugs me into the street, when I forget I'm on the sidewalk!
- A leash pulls me away from garbage (chicken bones, rotting food, glass) in the streets that can not only make me sick but can endanger my life
- A leash can protect me from other canines. I'm really friendly and I forget that every dog isn't like that . . .
- And a leash keeps me from other canines whose medical care may not be what it should be. . . . And as much as I like to meet my fellows, my health is too important to chance it with casual encounters.

So keep communication open and stay connected to your human being.
Insist on a leash and enjoy it!!!

RUFIO*

Raising Canine Consciousness

with
JP RUFIO

HI! It's already 1978 and I'm just sitting down to talk with you again . . . Sorry, it's been so long—I've been up to my ears (& tail) in business . . . and snow.

This New Year brings with it, what I call the "CLEAN UP AFTER ME" law which goes into effect this summer. I must admit to having mixed feelings about this new statute which requires my pet human to clean up my mess.

Strictly on the ecological side, of course it's right. When I was living in the country we could bury our mess in the earth (I still find myself instinctively trying to do that. Urban humans think I've been trained to wipe my feet . . . do you believe it!!) Anyway, once buried in the earth, it recycles itself. That of course can't happen in cement. Neither is other dirt eliminated as easily in the city. If you've walked in the gutter with your human . . . you know about side-stepping broken glass, drunk bodies, clothes, just junk. You know what it is to be tugged away from rotting Burger King, three day old pizza, disintegrating chicken bones . . . there isn't always room for us!

I guess the only attitude to have is this: that through this new but prejudicial law, we canines can set an example for our pet humans . . . and maybe . . . just maybe . . . they'll learn to clean up their mess too!

MORRIS ANIMAL FOUNDATION

531 GUARANTY BANK BLDG. • DENVER, COLO. 80202 • PHONE (303) 825-7255
Executive Director, Claude Ramsey; Equine Consultant, Wayne O. Kester, D.V.M., Brig. Gen

JP Rufio
c/o JP & Moonlight, Ltd.
101 West 12
New York, NY 10011

Dear Mr. Rufio (or may I call you JP?):

I just wanted to let you know that your friend Laura Nadworny has nominated you for Morris Animal Foundation's Dog of the Year Award. She sent us some material about your many activities and accomplishments, and you do indeed seem to be quite a dog.

We'll keep your biographical information on file and certainly consider you when the Dog of the Year is selected in December. In the meantime, watch those sidewalks!

Sincerely,

David Roos

CATS

JP's work for the Humane Society brought him into contact with a new form of life: cats. He penned a "Welcome" to the felines participating in the Madison Square Garden Annual Knickerbocker Invitational Cat Show known as the MEOW Show:

> "I've spent most of my life in the country. And out there the only cats I saw would elegantly glide by, stopping just long enough to grab at the butterflies or jump a tree—always aloof and seemingly unaware of me. And since I've been in New York, I haven't seen many cats at all . . .
>
> But as Spokesdog for the Humane Society of New York, I want to extend my paw in welcome to my cousin felines. We share many things: we need love, attention, proper medical care, good food and the freedom to express ourselves.
>
> When we are lucky we have wonderful pet human beings. It is my new job to speak out to help humans treat us well:
>
> ***To Raise Feline and Canine Consciousness***
>
> For now, WELCOME to the MEOW Show and . . . I'll be talking to you."
>
> —JP RUFIO

Cat people were suddenly beating down JP & MOONLIGHT's door begging for a t-shirt designed for their felines. JP did not know why, but he intuited that cats would not take to t-shirts the way dogs had. He decided to do a little research.

When friends invited Laura to their home for dinner, JP asked if he could go in her place. He usually wasn't that pushy, but these friends had a cat.

Throughout dinner JP never took his eyes off the cat. She was a real beauty. But as JP watched her

vamp about, he couldn't imagine her same action in a t-shirt. He ran a little test and discovered that if he held his paw on the tips of the cat's fur, the cat would react. JP and most of the dogs he knew, would not have noticed anyone touching the tips of their hair. They were all into body rubs.

JP got down on the floor and held the shirt out to slip over the cat's head. As if by magic, the shirt became suspended in midair. The cat darted in one end and out the other.

JP liked the cat's independence, but decided to give it another try. Down on all fours, JP purred back at the cat as he slipped it over her head and onto one paw and then the other. It was done. The cat was in the dog t-shirt.

The cat stood stiffly still. Rigidly she fell on her back. Her four paws were pointing straight up to the ceiling. "Rigor mortis" had set in. She was not moving. The shirt had blunted the ends of the cat's fur which, as JP had guessed, were the cat's sensory field. It was an ugly scene for such an elegant creature. JP had had enough. He gallantly ripped the t-shirt off her back. He was so ashamed to have demeaned her in that way.

Only a feline suffering from an identity crisis would consider wearing a t-shirt. Sure there would be cats seen in RUFIO's T-Shirts for Dogs, but they were cats led astray by their human masters. JP RUFIO refused to endorse a cat t-shirt . . . RUF!

"A Dreamer of Dreams . . ."
—Deuteronomy

Deep in JP's little poodle heart, he nurtured two special dreams which he believed were key to his success: a RUFIO's CANINE CLASSIC Ready-to-Wear Collection guest appearance on Johnny Carson's "Tonight Show" and a sale to super retailer JC Penney . . .

JP sat glued to the television. He had nested all his best rags and bones around him. The plate of cheese in front of him was going ignored. His right leg jutted out perpendicular to his side. JP's eyes were riveted on that screen in front of him. This was it. The t-shirts were going to be presented on "The Tonight Show's" annual Christmas gift show.

JP was hardly breathing. One gift after another was displayed, teased and attacked. The audience was loving it. JP was chomping at the bit. They brought on the gifts for pets. There it was, there it was. Oh, no, there it was: JP's white tuxedo t-shirt on a white poodle who had the shirt on upside down: the tuxedo design was on his stomach. Not only couldn't you see the tuxedo, you could hardly distinguish the white shirt from the white dog.

JP did not go to the rag. He went to the typewriter:

> ". . . I just want to take a minute to thank you for . . . choosing it as part of the "The Tonight Show" new product segment.
>
> But I must admit some disappointment with the shirt's presentation . . . Although RUFIO's T-shirt was designed for canines toasting the holidays, I think your poodle model may have been imbibing too early and too much: He had the shirt on upside down . . ."

Photography by Chuck Serra

JP slumped down gloomily. His dream had become a nightmare . . .

"The Tonight Show" was on the phone. Would JP make up some special t-shirts? They were going to put the RUFIO Collection on the show again.

JP could hardly contain himself. He had to go for walks every hour. It was all too unbelievable. The show sent him out a list of special sayings and JP got busy designing the shirts and having them screenprinted. He shipped them out within two weeks. And then he waited.

JP went crazy waiting to hear when the shirts would make their return engagement. Months went by. One Wednesday in March the call came through. The t-shirts would be on the show that Friday night. There was no time to go to Los Angeles. So JP did the next best thing. He called and told everyone he knew: JP RUFIO's brainchild was going to be featured on "The Tonight Show."

This time they did it right. Johnny Carson even pronounced his name correctly. He didn't show any of the special shirts but he did show the audience the JOG shirt, the bicycle jacket, and the tuxedo. When Carson held a picture of JP in his terrycloth tank top upside down, Ed McMahon astutely observed: "That dog does a lot of tricks!" The audience roared. JP was in heaven.

With his five minute claim to fame over, JP perched himself near the phone. He waited. Silence. Friday night and Saturday went by. The phone never rang. Was it possible that all thirty million "Tonight Show" viewers had been out partying on that particular Friday night?

Sunday morning the phone rang. It was the phone company. They were calling to inform JP that his phone was now working. It had gone out of order at 11:15 PM Friday night . . . RUF!

But there had been some important people watching the show that night, among them, a JC Penney merchandise manager. And as "The Tonight Show" is legendary to do, seeing the t-shirts in Johnny Carson's hands was confirmation enough to convince this buyer to place his order.

Negotiations began. JP was very nervous. This was the big time. This was what he had been working toward. JC Penney meant quantity. They also meant high quality at reasonable prices, a merchandising philosophy JP RUFIO wholeheartedly believed in. Besides, Penney's did not often endorse name designers.

JP could think of nothing else. He padded back and forth, back and forth. Compulsively he stuffed himself with cheese. He took out all of his rags and then ignored them. He could not stand this wait. He had been tough in these negotiations. He hoped he hadn't been too tough . . . maybe he hadn't been tough enough.

The doorbell rang. A messenger stood there with an envelope for JP. JP took it in his paws. He ripped it open with his teeth. For once he was at a loss for barks.

This was it. JP had done it. JC Penney was placing its order: $70,000 worth of RUFIO®s CANINE CLASSIC®, the Original T-Shirt for Dogs . . . RUF! RUF! RUF!

* * *

As JP meandered through the legs of his party guests, his head was filled with memories of the past as well as with his dreams for the future.

There was Danielle, who so desperately needed to be part of the latest fad, that she not only made a necklace from photos of JP for her ten month old daughter, but she had stuffed her kid into a RUFIO Sweatshirt for Dogs. As JP trotted by, he gave the little victim a dog biscuit.

Over there was Jane. For a time she had worked very hard for JP. She had even convinced her cat to wear a CANINE CLASSIC. But several weeks before, when Laura had been out of town, she had participated in some kind of orgiastic party and had left JP to starve for two whole days. JP padded over to her and bit her leg.

JP's nose dragged him back across the room. Some wonderful guest had left a chunk of cheese unguarded. JP went for it with both paws. In the middle of this heavenly indulgence, the guest book caught JP's eye. He flipped through it. It was filled with so many good wishes for his retirement. He became so absorbed, he forgot about the cheese.

JP looked up from the book. Tears of emotion welled in his eyes. He was proud of himself. Success was a warm puppy. He slurped some champagne which a guest had just spilled onto the floor next to him. This success wouldn't stop here.

So much life had touched him along the way. He had learned to love this "business" thing: the wheeling and dealing; the mental stretches; the fine line between going for quality and settling for sleaze. He had learned that you could be honorable and still succeed in business. You could be an original, you could do your own thing and still be a winner. And that you could work your tail off and still have fun.

Business and all its challenges would be a definite part of his future. But there were new things to reach for: a safari to Africa's wildlife preserves; a voyage with Greenpeace to follow the whales; a visit to China's endangered panda; an exploration of Mars and of course, he would have to learn everything he could about computers (any dog worth his eyeteeth would do that). JP planned to chronicle it all.

Guests were beginning to leave. JP saw them to the door, to bark his farewells. This was a bittersweet moment for JP. Tomorrow he would wake up in retirement, in the unknown. He looked up at Laura. She squatted down and hugged him. She read his mind: "We'll just have to start something new." He licked away her tears: "RUF."

> **"That a new beginning follows every ending is the course of heaven."**
> **—KU, "I Ching"**

MY SHADOW

I have a little shadow that goes in and out with me,
And what can be the use of him is more than I can see.
He is very very like me from the heels up to the head;
And I see him jump before me, when I jump into my bed.

The funny thing about him is the way he likes to grow—
Not at all like normal children which is always very slow;
For he sometimes shoots up taller like an india-rubber ball.
And he sometimes gets so little that there's none of him at all.

He hasn't got a notion of how children ought to play,
And can only make a fool of me in every sort of way.
He stays so close beside me, he's a coward you can see;
I'd think shame to stick to nursie as that shadow sticks to me!

One morning, very early, before the sun was up,
I rose and found the shining dew on every buttercup;
But my lazy little shadow, like an arrant sleepy-head,
Had stayed at home behind me and was fast asleep in bed.

—Robert Louis Stevenson
"A Child's Garden of Verses"

ABOUT THE AUTHOR

LAURA NADWORNY, a child of the sixties, proudly clutching her Masters in Broadcasting in one hand, JP RUFIO in the other; with professional experience as a writer-producer and clothes designer; and having absolutely NO interest in "Becoming a Business;" created the Original T-Shirts for Dogs and incorporated as JP & MOONLIGHT, ltd. Under her direction, JP & MOONLIGHT, ltd. successfully manufactured and marketed RUFIO®s CANINE CLASSIC® throughout the United States and Japan. Ms. Nadworny currently resides in New York City.